Billy the Cartwheeler

Reminiscences
by
W. Harrison Culmer
"The Last of the Dickens Boys"

*　*　*　*　*

The Scarecrow Press, Inc.
Metuchen, N.J.　　　1970

To Mrs. Josephine Vermilyea
Who insisted that it was my duty to make
known these memories and who inspired
me with the courage and ability to write
them, this book is affectionately dedicated.

Billy the Cartwheeler later in life

Preface and Author's Introduction

This book was written in America in the 1920s and early '30s by a man nearly 80 (he died in 1939 at the age of 87) who had emigrated from England nearly sixty years earlier. William Harrison Culmer, or "Billy the Cartwheeler," wrote of himself as "the only surviving member of what during the latter period of the life of Charles Dickens were known as the 'Dickens Boys.'" This book, which he wrote but never published during his life time, is a reminiscence of a few years as a little boy in London and friend of Charles Dickens. The following is the author's explanation of what it meant to be a "Dickens Boy" and may serve as an Introduction to his book.

It was the custom of Mr. Dickens to familiarize himself with the underworld haunts of London by keeping in touch with certain characters with whom he could ingratiate himself, the better to worm out intimate details of habits of living, tendencies of thought, idiom of language, aspirations, and no doubt slum attitudes toward law, order, and national life.

Among these characters, I think he took the most interest in, and likely received keener inspiration and perhaps more diversion for himself from boys, for he liked boys and because of his passionate democratic leanings he liked most the boys of the common people. Of these I am inclined to think he most liked or was most interested in incorrigible boys or at least pre-cocious boys. I was certainly one of these. These were "Dickens Boys."

Of such boys who attracted his atten-tion between 1840 and 1865, there must have been altogether approximately thirty or forty but never more than a few at a time. In my time, I have reason to believe there were from ten to fifteen of us but except on rare occasions we never appeared all together or even in groups so as to know each other or to know that we stood in the eyes of Mr. Dickens highter than any other boys. (One of these rare occa-sions I will later relate.)

It must be taken into consideration that in England in Dickens' time there were very few, almost no, authors who could or did descend to the level of the mind of a child in order to de-pict the romance and tragedy of boys' lives, par-ticularly those living in slums. Is it any wonder that all of that class who could read would avid-ly devour all of Dickens that pertained to their estate--and is it any wonder then that Dickens should use "his boys" to search out the qualities and the quantities of that estate?

He would no doubt frequently hear the common slang of the street, for example, but who would interpret it for him? He would, less frequently because it was guarded, hear thieves' jargon but how would he know what it was or how interpret it? He would have a curiosity to know many of the intimate things of slum living economy; yet could not himself witness this without unwarrantable intrusion. Nor could he learn at close hand of the methods of procurers, fences, evaders of law and stool pigeons. He could get much more of this from such as I than he could even from the far-reaching arm of the law, whose duty it was to know all about it. He no doubt obtained from us more detail of the sordidness and indecencies of that underworld than he would dare use or that I could bring here myself to relate, and much other detail, because of his nearing demise, he was deprived of an opportunity to use.

I must not permit the reader to gather the impression that he at any time abetted our acting as stool pigeons for him or persuaded us in any way to prowl the depths of vice. Some of us did this regardless of him. Also, Mr. Dickens had had more need for such methods of getting local color ten to twenty years before my time and when he was writing Oliver Twist, The Old Curiosity Shop, Little Dorrit, Great Expectations, and the like, than he had in my time, when his romancing work was steadily changing to statecraft.

Of all public characters whom boys could know he was best known; for by reason of the penny weekly serials of his popular works, which appeared in my time at every street corner at noon on Saturdays with a medallion portrait of himself in the upper left-hand corner, his visage was the best known of anyone's. I can recall his referring to us as "his boys" and in my own case I was introduced on an occasion as "one of my boys." I will explain why.

Contents

Chapter		Page

xiii

List of Illustrations

CHAPTER I

Mr. Dickens seems to have been aware
that the most insidious way of penetrating the minds
of common people with creedal belief was through
the common schools and that as all national
schools of that day were directly under the do-
minion of the National Established Church--the
Protestant Episcopal--it followed that education
was oligarchic and hierarchic and so, of course,
quite at dissonance with the liberal spirit and the
social equality for which he stood. Mention is
made of this here, as it has some bearing on my
recollection of him and to incidents I will relate.

The national school system was therefore
parochial, and to some extent compulsory, but it
was not free. Tuition was paid weekly as one
would pay rent, and attendance was conditional on
this Monday morning tax. The fee varied with
the grade; from 3d to 6d, I think, per week. I
became familiar with it only up to 4d.

At the time of which I am reporting [1860s]
and among my class of people, ordinary laborers
were paid two shillings and sixpence per day--the
contemporary equivilent to sixty cents in America;
and skilled mechanics, from four to six shillings--
a dollar to a dollar and a half. The reader
should understand that unemployment usually

averaged about forty per cent;   that women were
employed, if at all, at only the most menial
tasks; that drink exhausted at least a quarter of all
earnings; that rents, and all of us were renters,
took another quarter; and that families then, as
always among the poor, were large. Thus the
reader may realize what a burdensome tax was
the cost of education and yet how little of it
could be purchased.   The reader may then ap-
preciate, as we did, the need of free though
charitable schools and the blessing of Dickens'
passion for improving them.

       There were of course schools conducted by
all other religious orders and there were secular
schools for general or specific purposes which
were neither nationally nor parochially regulated,
but these were all either weekly fee schools or
on quarterly or annual payment terms.   In the
main these reached only to the grammar grades
and were comparable in rank and efficiency to
American grade schools.

       The cost of this preliminary education for
the poor, the hoi polloi of the people, was so
onerous as to be practically impossible and so
there had sprung up here and there, through the
public-spiritedness of neighborhood groups of
trades-people, what were known at first as "free
schools," then stigmatized as "charity schools,"
and finally contemptuously referred to as "ragged
schools."

       These usually were not regulated by any
cooperation or system among themselves but as
they were locally supported each had a local
board or committee to look after its affairs, to

employ its master, and to pay its expenses.   So
far as I can recall there was no law that interfered with or regulated the ragged schools in any
way.   They devised for themselves the amount
of money to be spent, the grades, or levels, to
be taught, which I think never extended beyond
the 3 R's (I am sure this was the limit at Magdalen), and they held examinations twice a year
to determine for themselves the proficiency of
their scholars and thus to whom awards should
be given.   These examinations were serious
functions to which parents and local dignitaries
were invited and to which most of them came.

What wonder then that an ideal that held out
such a promise of relief for the hungry poor who
clamored for a chance at education should reach
the sympathy and claim the championship of
Charles Dickens?

I will get more intimate about the Magdalen
Ragged School since it was about typical of all
of the others of that class.   I feel assured that
the system, its spirit, its influence, and its
freedom inculcated more thoroughly the rudiments
of a practical education in many millions of
children than did the contemporary, compulsive,
parochial system with all its tyrannous fees.

All that I shall relate here and more and
especially the particulars of what and how we
were taught and how thoroughly we were ground-
ed in what we did learn, of how much practical
use our learning was likely to be put, of the
proceedings of our half-yearly festivities, and
of my own part, was drawn from me in great

detail by Mr. Dickens in conversations and he
seemed not to be satisfied until the subject was
exhausted. This remembrance inclines me to
suppose that as Mr. Dickens was familiar with
the parochial system which had furnished himself
with part at least of his own limited education,
he was using this opportunity to visualize through
my mind the unorganized methods of the fee-less,
charitable variety and that he was doing this not
so much that he needed it for an aid in writing
fiction as that, at this time, he was engaged in
the more serious business of educational reform
in which he needed to know at first hand the facts
of the seamy side of the charity class of society.
The keen interest Mr. Dickens took led him to
visit Magdalen School, and no doubt he investiga-
ted other raggeds, but that would be after I had
left to go to work.

His manner toward me, part of my education too, inspired me with a descriptive form of
expression rather verbose for a child of my age
but he seemed to encourage this and my natural
precosity needed but slight stimulation. Where
I hesitated he would supply a hint or a word to
help me along.

The Magdalen Free School for Boys (pen-sketch by the author)

CHAPTER II

Magdalen Free School for Boys (its official title) was situated on Magdalen Alley, a narrow, cobble-paved, blind alley which opened on to Tooley Street. This was a small, filthy, and dark, river-front street paralleling the Thames which on the river side because of its wharves and ships was lined with ship chandlery supplying tar, oils, greases, hides, wool, tallow, and other naval stores and odoriferous things; and on the other side with ironmongery, ropes, anchors, chains, figureheads, and the like. The scum of the world came off the ships speaking the jargon of all nations and frequented the rat-infested taverns and dives, where drunken licenciousness and squalor was publicly revealed. Through this fearsome street two hundred to three hundred boys under the age of fourteen made their daily way to Magdalen Ragged School.

The building itself was put up while America was being discovered; while Shakespeare was busy modeling the English language; while Cortez was subjugating Mexico. It was set back from the alley about ten feet, was surrounded by a wall about twelve feet high, four feet thick, and surmounted with a heavy layer of broken jagged glass bottles which stood like daggers and spears and bayonets adamant against siege and

which defied scaling.   The school was one lofty
story high and it and the outer wall was of a
dull-red, hard-burned brick ten times the size of
modern brick and certainly more durable and laid
up with mortar that had defied and withstood the
ravage of centuries. The wall and the building
were each pierced with double gates six inches
thick of India teakwood, studded every few inches
with ebony or box-wood dowels. These gates
were large enough to admit a four-oxen van but
it was rumored that they had not been opened
for a century. Each gate had in it a postern
door of the same massive strength and these
were the only entry and egress for the building.

The building had been used, as the evidence showed us, successively through the centuries as a green-hide warehouse; as a hop
house; as a tan-bark mill; as a glue and ferti-
lizer works; and as a horse and cattle market;
and each had left its indelible stamp and especially its effluvia until at last by the blessing of God
it had emerged phoenix-like from its dead past,
amid a wilderness of human misery, to become
an oasis of education.

The interior of Magdalen was a single
room about sixty by a hundred feet. Its floor
was of oak timbers originally six inches thick
but now dreadfully uneven and showing the ravage of wear and the ruts of van tracks. There
was no ceiling. Looking upward was like looking at the vaulted heavens on a starless night
for the smoke of its various occupations of ages
ago had so sooted the underside of the roof that
it could hold no more shadows nor give a point
for either direct or reflected light to rest upon.

The roof was supported by heavy teak timbers
which spanned from wall to wall without posts
and were trussed by morticed and tenoned jack-
posts in an old English or Dutch fashion.   Outside, its roof surface was steep and covered
with slate slabs of enormous thickness.

Originally, the hall that was Magdalen
Ragged had had no windows but about a century
earlier for some reason (perhaps when it first
became a school) it had been pierced about eight
feet high with many small openings which were
glazed with little diamond-shaped panes feebly
permitting gleams of light to enter from above
the high wall without.   The forbidding aspect of
the broken-glass topping of this wall was indeed
the only thing we ever saw through these windows.

There was a cobble-paved courtyard about
ten feet wide that ran around the building, in the
two back corners of which were horrible specimens of out-houses.   Drinking water was obtained
from a pipe in the courtyard, water probably
drawn from the filthy river itself, and dispensed
from oak pails with heavy pewter ladles.   In the
court also was the scaffold of a cattle rack that
had formerly been used for shoeing oxen and
which was now a constant and cheerful reminder
of a gibbet.

Inside there were no desks.   The seats
were heavy mutilated plank timbers on round
strutting legs, arranged in tiers lengthwise of
the building with aisles between each tier.
Seated on these we did our work on our knees,
or, kneeling, did it on the seats.   That it was
uncomfortable and stunting to our poor bodies in

either case, I can testify.   But this cramping we
relieved at frequent intervals by marching around
the walls singing our tables by rote and chanting
in unison our spelling.

On the wall facing us was a long blackboard but so feebly did daylight enter the building
that all work upon it was performed gropingly and
perceived little.   One must remember that not
only was London, then as now, usually shrouded
in glooming fog, but that this was a time long
before coal-oil lamps, long before even paraffine
candles, when the only illumination possible was
by rushlight or tallow candles and dreadfully of-
fensive smoky torches which burned crude whale-
oil.

Facing onto the alley which ran curbless
and without pavement opposite the school, were
the rear views and fenced-in yards of the estab-
lishments on Tooley which contained the jetsam
of fittings from centuries back of England's proud
mistresses of the sea.   Museums of marine an-
tiquity.   Figureheads from the ships of Sir Francis
Drake, cannons off Lord Nelson's contra-Spanish
armada, enormous anchors, masts, and yard-arms
from which many a traitor and pirate had hung,
broken-up cabins of vessels long ago wrecked but
showing still past splendor and gilt.

Tucked in among these were small shops
catering to the envious desires and small purchas-
ing powers of us boys.   One I shall ever remember had its dirty show window arrayed with tempt-
ing sweets that whetted the appetite and invited patronage, but made a specialty also of
rattan canes in such nicely assorted lengths and

girths that they seemed to measure degrees of
punishment, and these, ominous of impending
thrashings, were neatly interspersed with the
brandy balls, jujubes, and sugared walking
sticks. The shop was distinguished as the official purveyer, to our school, of this Inquisitorial
instrument of torture and the schoolmaster, with
a disposition of generosity toward increasing his
patronage there, and with a fine sense of ironical
humor, would on occasion dispatch an offending
and sentenced culprit across the alley, with a
farthing, to purchase and bring back his selection
of implement for the punishment. In retaliation
for this barbarous design, such a messenger
often deftly arranged on the way back that the
cane should split or break at the first blow. Or,
he had been known to take to his heels with the
farthing.

In my own case on one occasion, the
ugly, wizened little dwarf, the shopkeeper, who
ought to have been on a treadmill instead of in
such a nefarious trade, confidentially and mysteriously instructed me that if I would contrive
to get a hair out of my shock head and lay it
across my hand just as I obligingly held it out
and just before the blow came, it would split the
cane end-to-end at the first blow. I rehearsed
the trick carefully during the brief period of preparation and then presented my hand like a Spar-
tan.

But it didn't work. In actual operation
it was a grievous and painful disappointment.
The man was a double-cross villain.

But, dismal and appalling, dangerously

unsanitary, and comfortless as it was, the
Magdalen Ragged School was a blessed philan-
thropy of the neighborhood tradesmen and an
opportunity--it could scarcely be called an in-
spiration--for millions such as I to get the
rudiments of an education.   And it was all the
school education I ever got.

CHAPTER III

At these free schools there were no religious requirements for entrance and little of any other kind. If a parent brought a child and promised to be responsible for its any act of destruction, it was enrolled.

The schoolmaster was given absolute authority as to the curriculum. He could refuse admission, he could expel, and punish, promote, and reward. Unlike the sectarian and parochial schools, no distinguishing uniform was required. On the contrary, we could arrive bare-footed and bare-headed and were, in fact, mostly bare-faced. Clean hands and faces were insisted upon and the absence of these occasioned the most painful disciplining and a resort to the hydrant in the yard.

Free slates, spelling books, copy books, and arithmetics were provided but nothing else was. Instruction was mostly by rote with the entire school in a single class. The blackboard, though so dimly in view of the whole room, was freely used. Not even the primer of grammar was taught; reading was oral and often in unison. Arithmetic studies ended with long division and tables were recited orally. Writing, begun with the pot-hooks, rapidly developed to good Spen-

cerian; indeed our ragged boys became the best
penmen of the nation.   The limits of age at this
school were over nine and under fourteen.   Most
of us were graduated or left for life's hard work
before we were fourteen.   I left at eleven and a
quarter.

Into our dismal building, after the two
hundred and fifty of us were assembled in the
alley and courtyard, we marched goose-step
fashion at the clanging of a bell in the hands of
the "monitor," or head boy.

After assembling in the courtyard, the
postern door in the out-gates was locked with a
lock like that of a medieval fortress and with a
key that was a load to carry.   When this period
arrived the premises assumed every appearance
and feeling of a dungeon.   There was no further
ingress or egress at the outer gate until dismissal except when there came the known peculiar tinkling which heralded the master or a
trustee.   Late scholars were taboo.

I have explained that the cost of maintain-
ing Magdalen fell to charitable neighboring shop-
keepers.   The budget thus devised from their
contributions was always so small that after
meeting other expenses there was little left for
paying a teacher.   The board of trustees therefore had to employ either a volunteer teacher
with funds of his own, which did not usually work
out harmoniously, or, as in our case, a teacher
who had some other occupation with which to help
support himself.   That is how we came to get
Mr. Harding (bless his soul) who was also a
letter carrier and who was obliged to make a

mail delivery in the morning, which occupied his
attention until ten o'clock, and another delivery
in the afternoon, which obliged him to leave
school at three o'clock. And so, the opening exercises, which consisted of the national anthem
and the Lord's Prayer, and the closing exercises:
"Britains never, never, never, never, never,
never shall be slaves" and some calisthenics,
were supervised by the monitor, a position of
privilege to which every boy aspired, especially
as some member of the board would be likely to
drop in for praise or criticism of these exercises. It was a coveted and desperatively
striven-for promotion, to get to be monitor, as
will be seen later.

In his position as schoolmaster, Mr.
Harding received twenty-one pounds (about one
hundred dollars) per year and there were no
perquisites. He was a little man of about fifty
years, well educated, with a fine intellectual
appearance, and married with a grown-up family.
He liked boys and cleverly managed them; he
commanded their respect and when needs be,
thrashed them. This duty--painful to him--was
a frequent one. Often he had to face and punish
a small army of us at once and on such an occasion a curious thing happened, occasioned I
think by the common sympathy of all of us toward
him because of his uniformly just and cheerful
leadership.

Thus--when he would be arrayed against
numbers or even with a single one who was
likely to assault him, an equal number of us,
or more, without concert or prearrangement and
certainly not with his connivance, would quietly

disengage ourselves from the mass and surround
the scene of conflict.   Then, in the event of retaliation by a bully or by a crowd the defenders
took a hand in it and did something.   Oh my,
what they did do then!   But the fact that this
retaliation was nearly assured, and that the
master was nearly always sure to come out of
it victorious either by his own prowess or by
our help, prevented the beginnings of many a
bloody fracas.   I was such a little runt that I
was of but small use in the bodyguard but I did
valiant service as a teaser on the side lines.

The rattan cane about the girth of a thick
lead pencil was the master's most effective
weapon and the palm of the victim's hand, the
most favorable arena for punishment.   Caning
extended, however, to other and more vulnerable
parts of the anatomy, and often produced upstanding
students.   Corporal punishment by a master at
that time, instead of being prohibited, was expected and even demanded by parents.   In some
cases, I think, we were sent to school in order
to get there a licking that we had earned at home.
This fact brought with it its dangers of mutiny
and this in turn produced the voluntary bodyguard.

I remember one occasion, because of the
alliterative name of the culprit, when corporal
punishment had a different effect at a boy's home.
Richard Richardson, who lived on Richardson
street, and who was a large, strong boy, the son
of a large, strong Irishman, had received a well-
deserved thrashing by the master at recess and
had run home blubbering to his father.   He, exasperated by the welts on his precious son,
dragged him hasteful back to the school intent on

man-handling the master.

"Aire yez the gaffer 'ere?" asked he, glowering at the little teacher.

"I have that pleasure, Mr. Richardson," said our master facing the irate Irishman, "if you mean the master."

"An' did a little runt like yez lick me big b'y like that?" pointing to the fast blackening eye and stripes on his hands and arm. "Whut fer?"

"For calling me a blankety-blank," replied the master, mentioning a provocative epithet of the day.

"Unh," said the man, "an did yez do it all alone?" shifting his glowering eyes to take in the twenty biggest of us that crowded the scene intent and quivering to get in the fray.

"Yes," the schoolmaster said.

"You bet 'e did," shouted we; "do it ag'in too!"

The master raised his hand for silence. The look of rage Mr. Richardson wore gradually turned to a comical expression and broadened and broadened until it enveloped his whole face. Then grasping his boy by the collar he shook him as a terrier would a rat and dragged and kicked him all the way to the alley. Richard did not appear again for several days but we found out that his father had also licked him, first for the insult to the master, and second for letting a smaller man than himself lick him.

Love and respect from such barbarous
boys as we were, drawn from the crudest,
cruelest, and most vicious environment of London, could hardly be expected significantly to
have leavened our mass attitude toward discipline. And yet I am sure that in Magdalen
these affections did materially help. We had our
rebellions, our bloody fights, and our pitched
battles, but when the wounded were patched up
we found Mr. Harding cheerfully in command
and kindly disposed.

I must not leave the subject of my school
without first introducing myself more familiarly.
At nine years of age I was sent to the Nelson
Parochial Primary, ostensibly to comply with
lawful requirements but in reality to keep me
off the streets. For I had by then not only developed into a regular street gamin--an apache
of the alleys--but, an urchin professional, in
that I had become the champion athlete among
boy cartwheelers and earned (literally picked up)
more than all the other bread winners of my
family combined. I had been training for this
since I was three. At first it had been regarded
as cute and clever and I acquired great proficiency. Later, after it become a vice and was
forbidden, I practiced it in secrecy away from
home and in dangerous company. Cartwheeling
was the precarious occupation of turning sideways handsprings running alongside, and at the
speed of, the omnibuses and post chaises to pick
up from London's slime the coins that passengers threw off for my reward. It was unlawful
thus to expose myself to this fearful risk of

Billy the Cartwheeler in action (pen-sketch by the author)

street accidents; it was unsanitary; it brought
me into dreadful companionship and fierce fighting; it was opposed by the family and at length
I was banished as stated to Nelson's Primary
at 3d per week.

I was already ahead of this primary for
I had atteneded dear old Mrs. Deighton's kinder-
garten, off and on, since I was five and could I
not read and write and figure better than any kid
at Nelson's?   I knew this and so was persuaded
by some boys I knew in Magdalen to switch
schools; and, as I did not have to dress up to
go there nor pay threepence per week, I easily
coaxed my mother to take me there for enroll-
ment.   I have thanked God for that ever since;
for all the scholastic training I have had; all
the self-reliance; all the ethical foundation I
have, I got at Magdalen.

Here I diligently pored and slaved with
ne'er a truancy nor desire for it, but with many
a fight, until the following year, when it was decided at home that I must quite school and go to
work, my help now being a necessity in the
family because of the emigration to America of
the two oldest children.   This decision I brought
to the master at Magdalen, who, being rather
fond of me, contrived to set aside precedence
and precedent and appoint me monitor for the
remainder of the term.

This promotion ordinarily would have
provoked bitter opposition and persecution from
other aspiring, and older, boys but this was
offset in my case, first because it was announced that my czardom was to last only a

month, and second and more particularly, because my athletic tricks: tumbling, handwalking,
cartwheeling and so on, and my willingness to
teach the other boys these tricks, had won from
them a rude sort of admiration.

But there was another reason for this
peaceful permission for my promotion. I was
a sailor boy. I had been to sea with my father,
who was a skipper. I had visited foreign parts:
Ostend, Zeabruge, Amsterdam, Calais, Le Havre,
Oporto, Lisbon, and even to far-off Marseilles,
Naples and Nice. I had met them furriners; I
could talk in nautical language; I could box the
compass, I could shoot the sun, and, what was
more to the point, I could tell amazing stories
about these things. It really became for them
an honor rather than a condescension to suffer
my promotion.

More important, and more far-reaching
in its results perhaps, was the fact that having
been obliged to take charge of the singing exercises during this month of authority, I enlarged
their scope and gave evidence that I had skill and
training in this direction also. This advantage
will appear later on.

Also, there was a largess that went with
this promotion. Under a long-standing rule, the
trustees of Magdalen were obligated to use, for
every boy who worked his way up to be monitor
and left as such, its influence to secure for him
his first wage-earning situation, provided he
needed such help and applied for it. In my case,
with boundless ambition and optimism the application was made early with roseate expectations

on my part of at least an ambassadorship to
America, but if need be, a seat in parliament,
or, scaling downward, a barristorship, or a
job as a singing master, or even a fight pro-
motor's position--for this last was at the time
most in the public eye. As it turned out there
was a need for a large fund of the good sense
born of experience to be satisfied with anything
I could get.

CHAPTER IV

At the time of my graduation from
Magdalen there must have been a terrible in-
sufficiency of jobs, or, because of my small
stature, I did not seem to fit in anywhere.
Mayhap fate intended my agile mind be made to
fit into some dreadful experiences. At any rate
the only billet available was as a lather boy in a
a half-penny barber shop in the New Cut. My
master here was a brutal, drunken sot who fit
his surroundings harmoniously and fitted me into
a profound disgust of him, his occupation, and
his associates.

And yet this place, singularly enough,
was begun as a philanthropic institution for
bread-line customers who were drawn from the
coster fraternity of the New Cut; the drovers
and slaughterers from the Smithfield market;
the skinners and tanners from Bermondsey and
the professional beggars of the Mint and Seven
Dials--aliens of every clime--whose earnings
could not stand the strain of the three-penny
shops. Missus Dan Ward really was the phi-
lanthropist. She was the owner of the premises
and lived on the upper floors where I had a tiny
hall bedroom which was filthy dirty and without
any of the comforts of home to which I was accustomed and where I was fed from the scrapings

and leavings of her own table. She supported
the business--which was a losing venture--from
funds of her own, ostensibly as a charitable institution but chiefly in an effort to reform her
husband--which was also a losing venture.

A ha'penny barber shop must necessarily
be located among the poorest and densest population and so this one was quite in place in the
New Cut--not only the poorest but also the vilest
locality in all London. The shop was reached
by mounting four steps of what had once been a
residence. Through the center of the shop
ranged three rows of common, rush-bottom,
kitchen chairs in different stages of unrest.
Along the walls were ragged, carpet-covered,
plank benches for waiting customers, above
which on rollers hung public towels in various
conditions of wet, blood-stained decrepitude.
The floor, wickedly rotten and unsanitary, was
sand-strewn and on this, from morning until
night, fell the assorted shades of hirsute adorn-
ments from the heads of its penurious customers.
These perquisites was scraped up with a fine
rake nightly by the lather boy (me) and sold to
mortar mixers. Nightly also the towels, or
such of them as remained serviceable, were
boiled and washed in a copper kettle in a flea-
infested cellar, by this same boy, and hung in
the cellar to dry for duty on the morrow.

Tied to stout cords and hanging alongside each towel were heavy horn combs in dif-
fering stages of serration and accumulated bac-
teria. These also were boiled at night after the
towels but with an addition of concentrated potash
which was supposed to be death to all sorts of

(Missus) Dan Ward's Ha'penny Barber Shop (pen-sketch by the author)

vermin life. These, with the exception of prize-
fight pictures on the walls, comprised all of the
appointments of the shop. It had no mirrors,
it was lighted by smoky kerosene lamps, and it
was unregulated by any sanitary laws.

In such a shop, for every six chairs was
assigned a barber and to every twelve chairs, a
lather boy. The barbers were itinerants sup-
plied daily by an agency on a standing order.
On Saturdays and Sundays there was always a
customer waiting-list or a special requisition
for an extra barber. Since one or more of them
were likely to get too drunk for action before
night, a requisition for specials was of daily
occurrence.

A barber brought his own tools, when
they were not in pawn, in which latter case the
agency would lend him a set at threepence per
day. He began work at 7 a.m. on the basis of
three bob (75¢) if he remained sober all day,
or at 2d per hour for his sober time if he got
drunk or was fired. He was not regarded as a
good journeyman if he did not average twenty-
five haircuts at a penny and fifty shaves at a
ha'penny per shift. These were trade standards
and were mutually satisfactory when master and
barber remained sober; if either of them, drunk
or sober, disputed these terms, there was a
fracas in which everybody was welcome.

The customer's business was to watch
for his turn from the sidelines, which if usurped
was to be fought for, and tó be seated one behind the other three feet apart so that his foot,
aimed at the lather boy or the barber, could not

reach the forward chair.   This was necessary
to prevent sanguinary accidents.   After being
served, indicated by his chair being tilted forward to land him on his feet, the customer re-
paired to the side-lines to wipe his face on the
roller towels among the other stains.

The lather boy's business was to carry
a low stool, in his left hand if he happened to
be right-handed, or reversed if he were left-
handed, from chair to chair, mount the stool,
jab back the sitter's head, warn him to keep his
mouth shut under penalty, then lay on the lather
and rub it in (with raw and bleeding fingers
from countless stubbles), hurrying to keep ahead
of his pace-maker, the barber behind him,
listening meanwhile to smothered oaths from the
clients and the most motley jargon and indecencies from everyone else, waiting with trepidation
all the while for a kick or a box on the ears
from the master if he dared to complain or
whimper.

The barber's business was to follow up
the lather boy and hound him if he were slow or
did not leave a nice creamy surface for attack,
to keep his razors just sharp enough to get by
between the customer and the master, to make
one comprehensive all-around swoop of such
parts of the face as the lather boy had lathered,
and last, to tip the chair forward and holler
"Next!"

There were small, square rags derived
from old clothes which the barbers used as
wiping rags and which when sufficiently used
were thrown in a corner.   It was the lather

boy's business on Sunday afternoons to wash these
and hang them to dry in the shop, which was
thus given a truly speckled appearance, after
which he had the rest of the day off to go home
to mother to have his poor bleeding hands comforted and kissed and cried over; but better yet,
a promise of a mother-cooked dinner on the day
off coming Wednesday.

A lather boy did not, I think, tell his
mother all of his miseries nor half of them;
each was on the lookout for a bettering of fortune.

I cannot write this, I cannot think back
to this experience, without a gasp of horror at
the memory of the nauseating food, the filthy
bed, the lewdness and the indecency of it all;
for which I got three shillings a week, plus
board, bed, and tips--and you can imagine how
few of these. The only bright ray being that
each week all but threepence of the money went
to America and most of the Wednesdays to Mr.
Dickens.

CHAPTER V

But this narrative being of Dickens and the London slums, I must not leave this neighborhood without telling the reader more about the New Cut.

Its "newness" was at least a hundred years old. Tradition and rumor had it that an original intention had been to name it Westminster Drive. Perhaps this is so but no maps extant from any date give so lofty an appellation. If the lines of it were extended it would have intersected Westminster Road, after crossing Southwark and Blackfriars Roads, which gives color to this tradition. Rumor also had it that something more was done to it at about the time of the succession of the Queen, when it was proposed to call it Victoria Place. By the fact that the Victoria Theatre was erected on it at about that time and still remains its most conspicious feature, this rumor is lent color. But New Cut it began and continued, and New Cut it will probably be to the end of time.

From the south bank of the Thames River to about a mile away from it to the south, is Southwark Borough. As near as I can remember it was also bounded on the west by Westminster; on the east, by Bermondsey; and on the south,

by Kensington.   Between it and Bermondsey ran
the Borough Road which ended at London Bridge.
This most prominent thoroughfare, fairly wide in
places, ran in different curves and tangents and
took on a different name at each, but in general
was known as "the Borough" from end to end.
Conspicuously on the lower reaches of this road
was St. George's Church and its cemetery.   A
little distance behind the church was, and perhaps is yet, the old Marshalsea Debtors Prison
that Mr. Dickens had reasons for knowing very
well, as did I for different reasons.

Within this area and hard by the river
margin and between the London and the Southwark bridges was the Borough Market devoted
especially to the wholesaling of agricultural products.   To this market there came up the river
from the market gardens of Kent and Essex
wherries, barges, lighters, scows, and other
hand-driven craft, and sailing vessels of sloops,
schooners, and cutters, and steam packets from
the nearby foreign shores of The Netherlands,
Belgium, France, Portugal, Spain, and Italy, in
endless procession and laden with green and dairy
food for the Borough and with fish for Billingsgate
which was opposite and beneath the bridge.

And to this market from every greengrocer, fruiterer, and caterer and from every
quarter of all London, came every conceivable
sort of vehicular conveyence: big high-sided vans
drawn by four horses or by two horses, or one,
or donkey carts, push carts, or even wheelbar-
rows, but mostly one or two-man push carts.
The congestion from all of this--especially in
the early morning hours--was terrific for such

narrow streets, lanes, and alleys as I have described.   To add to the congestion was the tram
traffic of the railways from all other parts of
England, each bringing its quota of perishable
food.

To visualize all this, the reader must
forget everything else he knows of modern
transportation.   Nothing today in America or in
England remotely compares with it.   Except for
a feeble effort that had been made to keep open
a thoroughfare between the bridges leading across
Southwark and Blackfriars into Westminster, the
streets were all narrow, crooked, cobble-paved,
very rough, and befouled.   Some were mere
lanes that fed the streets or muddy alleys that
fed the lanes and all were littered and badly
lighted or murky with no light at all.   For a
radius of a mile from this market were a poly-
glot of nationalities, garbed in fashions of all
strata and caste from Greenland's mountains to
India and the East.

In this ill-smelling human maze and
verminous wilderness the authorities, years
and years ago, attempted a reform by demolish-
ing and cutting through a wide modern street to
bring more air and sunshine into the heart of
the district.   This improvement was begun in
the middle and worked both ways and then for
some reason that no one living knows anything
about, it stopped and this wide street portion
remaining--the New Cut--is approached, or was
up until my day, only by the same old narrow
streets and alleys, in one of which was (Missus)
Dan Ward's Half-Penny Barber Shop.

Because of the curtailing of the improvement which I have mentioned, the New Cut was
more of a court than a thoroughfare. It was
entered on either side by the numerous small
cuts, arteries and veins of the old system,
which sucked in some of this openness to their
own inner darkness and congestion. It is
flanked by no imposing buildings of modern design. Of those of vintage, the Victoria Theatre,
lovingly, the "Old Vic," was the most conspicuous. This vast building in Dickens' time and
mine was, in spite of its sordid environment,
the seat of enchantment, the fairyland of desire,
the home of pantomine, the wonderland of illu-
sions. Five thousand of us nightly fought for
entrance and other thousands of us milled around
all evening outside the stage doors, amazed and
excited. We witnessed between acts the exits of
princesses, courtiers, kings and generals, hangmen
and bluebeards, harlequins, columbines and
clowns, sprites and elfins, goblins and gnomes,
and all the other creatures of fancy, who
swarmed in tinsel and grease-paint to the wide
sidewalk edge, there to regale--under flaring,
smoky torches--luscious pickled whelks, peri-
winkles in butter, roasted chestnuts ten-a-penny,
hot buttered muffins, pease pudding penny-a-
slap, fried sole a la france, blood sausage
smothered with gravy, or red hot monkey nuts,
all of these condiments and many others being
dispensed by costermongering Cockneys, Irish,
Scots, and Jews, with jargon yells: dozens of
eats, hundreds of slogans, thousands of patrons,
stuffing as though starved.

All the world goes to London. All London went to the "Vic"; for high and low, rich

and poor, everyone loved a pantomine, or right-
ly, a kaleidoscopic circus of vaudeville, ballet,
and opera.   The "Old Vic" was reported to be
the largest and best pantomimic in England, if
not the world.   Its stage was wide and deep,
permitting vast numbers of performers.   Admission was priced to suit the patrons, from a
shilling at the top of "queen's heaven," to five
pounds for a royal box in front.   Only the nobility or gentlemen of parts could occupy the
boxes, with fashionably dressed people in the
stalls and dress circle, women with escorts in
the first gallery, and the hoi polloi in the
"uppers. "

        A pantomime would be months in the
making, then burst forth with scintillating splendor on Christmas Eve, run for months, perhaps
the whole year and go out in glory.   The "Old
Vic's" repertoire included within my memory
"Cinderella," "Sinbad the Sailor," "Puss in
Boots," "Arabian Nights," and "Blue Beard."

CHAPTER VI

Within the square mile of area I am describing, which still did not take in all of Southwark, more than a quarter of a million of Lon -
don's worst population dwelt. It was the harbor
of the fruit and vegetable venders, the street
mendicants, professional (and disguised) beggars,
garroters, sneak thieves, pick-pockets, counter-
feiters, melters, burglars, murderers, fences,
harlots, and procurers. There were the young
apprenticed to vice and the old practicing and
teaching it. It was the warehouse of iniquity,
the executive offices of which and the pecuniary
profiteers of which and the business exchange of
which were not here, not visibly here, but more
likely in high and mighty places, unsuspected.

Within this area was the notorious
"Seven Dials" where converged a number of
crooked lanes that threaded off into dark and
sinister alleys emitting at last into daylight
business streets. This vile nest, with others
similar, was of course patrolled by police reg-
ulars but these came in contact only with exposed and minor infractions of the law. It required well trained detectives, mostly plain-
clothes men: sleuths "to that manor born " and
bred through underground experience, disguised
linguists of thieves' slang, who consorted with

50

criminals in order to apprehend them.

This was not a region that had degener-
ated from a more respectable and genteel
class--as other slums of London have.   On the
contrary, it had been manufactured to order;
evolved, so to speak, by the needs and the will
of just the class of beings that occupied it.

From appearances, the ground of Seven
Dials was originally a swamp from the river
overflow and infested with reptile and rodent.
Then the human river-rat, the beach-comber,
and the burrowing fugitive took possession.
Later, those in river commerce improved its
margins and swarmed over it without survey or
system, following animal trails, tow-paths, and
lines of least resistance.   Building at first was
on stilts, then, as the centuries passed, there
rose structures with more substantial footings
and two, three, and sometimes four stories of
enduring material.   The ground, or original surface, mostly bog, had risen by its own debris,
or from fill from the outside until at last, as
I knew it, the ground surface was at the height
of the second stories, leaving the lower story
underground.   The rising of the ground had not
however raised the tenants and their occupations
nor their moral aspirations with it.   The same
grog shops, the same taverns, the same inns
and lodgings which began their days and are
ending their years in vice and pestilence are
now one story underground.   The Fagans, the
fences, the refugees, and the suspect, like rats,
continued in their natural element.   There were
many other pestholes of like character in Limehouse, Shoreditch, Whitechapel, Ratcliffe Highway

and the Dock district, but I have described perhaps the worst and the largest.

Without doubt the introduction of modern
public utilities together with the civic pride recently taken on by this chief city of the world
has obliterated much of this squalor but in our
day an outsider would not have ventured to explore what I have described.   One necessarily
had an experienced conductor.   The same was
true for Mr. Dickens, and who more willing,
more capable, and more imaginative than the
boy of experience whom he might happen on for
this purpose?   One should not be led to suppose
that he suggested any such loathsome enterprise
as sleuthing in his behalf, but to find the information already acquired was acceptable to
his needs.   And how he did pump it out of us.
His works indicate that he had done a bit of
sleuthing for himself in his younger and less
dignified days, learning thereby the need of it
and using it afterwards to most clever advantage.

And I think he would agree with me that
the same cunning subtlety and perseverance
that is used by these slum professors in their
expert lines of crime, including training and
debauching the bright children of the slums in
their unlawful crafts, would, if developed by
morally trained educators of the state give many
of them remarkable character.   For as a rule
these children were bright, not erudite of course,
but shrewd, logical, crafty, and ambitious, and
in their way also, courageous and daring.   They
would have if properly trained, made good lead-
ers--better than most in higher strata--in an
emergency, in a scrimmage, in pioneer life,

or as soldiers: in anything, in fact, requiring
sudden decisions.   For the incessant struggle
for self-preservation which is theirs from birth
until adolescence has made them so.   It was in
this sort of reform, the useful training of slum
children, that Mr. Dickens was engaged.   His
optimistic vision was that some day it would be
achieved and that there was no path that brings
such richness and glory in life as whole-hearted
devotion to human welfare.

CHAPTER VII

A decade before the time I am describing all England had been excited over a most ambitious enterprise, that of entertaining the whole world with a great International Exposition, the first world's fair. The proposal had interested all classes of commerce and art within the kingdom and all other nations had participated in it.

It was now proposed to celebrate the tenth anniversary of this event and on a much larger scale; so much larger and so much more magnificent that the original Hyde Park buildings and grounds, which had come to be known as the Crystal Palace, were found to be inadequate for the purpose, beside which a fire had recently destroyed much of the Palace. And so, a site of three hundred acres (a part of which was donated from Royal domain) was secured at Sydenham six miles south of the former site, and in Kent. On this a much larger and more enduring Crystal Palace was erected. Two hundred and fifty acres were used for the buildings, botanical gardens, zoological parks and other features; the Palace itself covered eighteen acres. It was regarded when completed as the most perfect example of modern architecture and of modern construction methods in

the world. New lines of transportation, by rail,
tram, and highway, were laid to it from every
direction which fortunately brought the necessity
of razing many of the slums, including a part
of the district I have been describing, and was
the beginning of a greater era of civic improvement than London had ever before attempted.

This little bit of history is related only because it leads again to Mr. Dickens. As the
time approached for the opening of the new
Crystal Palace it was proposed that among other
attractions of a big nature, a choir of twenty-
five thousand London school children should be
selected and trained to sing a concert of national
hymns and anthems before the Queen and other
royal patrons. The proposal received Her Majesty's most gracious approval. Naturally, any
effort that would increase and intensify the loyal
fervor of twenty-five thousand intelligent boys,
as these boys were by reason of their careful
selection, boys who in the next decade or two
would be stepping into the shoes of the nation's
managing forces, was a project deemed well
worth while, to say nothing of its effect on the
military strength and efficiency of the future.

Now it was rumored that this idea of a
boys' choir of such magnitude and for such a
purpose originated with Mr. Dickens, and who
was there more likely than he, under all the circumstances, to conceive it, and who more
thoroughly able than he to organize and put it
into effect? But whether this was so or not,
it is certain that he became the chairman of a
large and titled commission to bring it about.

From out of this body came a sub-com-
mittee to determine the manner of selection of
such a multitude of juvenile talent and the
methods of training it.

In due time this committee reported to
the commission and among other things it re-
commended that the boys should be obtained by
drafting a pro-rata number from each of the
parochial schools of London and its suburbs.
This proposal instantly brought violent opposition from Mr. Dickens who always stood staunch
for the privileges of the lowly and the war on
this question waxed hot for quite a while, Mr.
Dickens contended that the chief purpose of the
whole project was that of instilling patriotic
fervor and loyalty in the hearts and minds of
all English boys, not only Church of England
boys, and that all other sectarian and especially
free and charity schools should and must be
equally included in the draft.

Mr. Dickens won out. Incidentally,
through the newspapers a lot of enthusiasm and
inspiration was preached to the English nation.
We poor "ragged boys" were given the impression that good Queen Victoria herself had decided the question in our favor.

Here was exemplified the whole heart
and soul of this great man Dickens, his democratic instincts, his moral courage, his passionate sympathy toward the weak and humble
as well as his diplomatic and executive skills,
and his unselfish nature. It would have been
very easy for him to acquiesce to the committee
report and permit this privilege to go with its

prestige to aristocracy but although it was a
minor matter it instantly enlisted his fighting
instinct.

But there was a real reason which mili-
tated against Mr. Dickens' contention. This
was at the time of Fenianism, a name given to
a certain political revolt that opposed the Pope.
It was led by the zealous liberal patriot Garibaldi but was believed to have been instigated
in America. It really did not concern England
much but as it was a semi-religious quarrel
with Roman Catholics on one side and mostly
Protestants on the other it was inevitable that
those of either faith who dissented should take
a hand in it.

As there were as many Irish Catholics
in England as there were in Ireland and as the
Irish in London were on principle always anti-
government, and as there were more Irish boys
than there were Irish men and much more bellig-
erent, and as these boys, being Roman Catholic,
could not be Protestant Episcopal and as the
parochial schools must be Protestant, it followed
that Catholic boys would be against Fenianism.
And they decidedly were.

It was axiomatic that an Irishman couldn't
fight with his fists because he had always his
shillelagh and it was axiomatic that an English-
man couldn't fight with a club because he had
his fists; but they had to fight somehow because
of Garibaldi offending the Pope. And so in New
Cut we went to it, from babes at the breast to
one-leg-in-the-gravers, and it waxed hot and
everywhere. Schoolboys and especially boys of

the slums were the most vicious. The slogan
was, "Aire yez for Garibaldi or the Pope?"
If you happened to answer favorably while the
other was clutching your wind-pipe without, perhaps, knowing anything whatever about the con-
troversy--all right; if you didn't, well, the
memory of it is painful to recall.

It was well-known to the commission
that the worst offenders in these running battles
were the parochials and the raggeds. The commission knew also, and were worried, that by
any process of selection there would still be a
division between the two and that the disharmony
resulting therefrom must necessarily mar the
dignity of the occasion. For all that Mr.
Dickens won out anyway and the levy for boy
singers included some of us from Magdalen.

So it is from joyful memory I recall that
this test of democracy turned out in regard to
New Cut boys to be the most admirable, leavening, ameliorating, and saving propaganda toward
peace that was ever tried. Not only among the
boy singers was it a great success, but to a
great extent the Queen's Choir triumph affected
the apaches of the streets and the adult population too.

Of course I was, at the time, too young
to have reasoned this out from cause to effect
but somehow we had received the impression
that, but for Mr. Dickens and the Queen, we
ragged boys would have had no part in that choir
and it is easy to conceive how this increased
our loyalty to our Queen and our respect for our
defender.

So, the draft on the schools was made
including Magdalen and all charity schools.   It
embraced only boys with childish voices between
nine and fourteen who could pass a prescribed
test.

It reached Magdalen just at the time I
was made monitor.   Christmas was near and
because of this poor Mr. Harding--as letter-
carrier--was too rushed to give any attention to
his duties as schoolmaster, the school was in
training for its annual examinations, and the
board of trustees, mostly shopkeepers, were
very busy with their holiday trade: all events
conspired in making the monitor, as head of
the scholars, responsible for the selection of
our choir quota, and he was ordered to attend
to it.   It took a week of mass singing, pitched
battles and drawn fights, and a lot of elimina-
tion, but in the end harmony, and twenty-five
winners, were selected and certified for what we
now regarded as the most momentous event of
our lives.   There is only this to add, that
curiously but with becoming modesty, little
Billy the monitor found himself at the head of
his school quota.

All of my family since before my birth
and before our removal to London from a quiet
village in Kent had been bending every energy
toward immigrating to the colonies, either Australia or Canada, but it happened that my parents
had become converted to the faith of the Latter
Day Saints and consequently we were all being
trained in the tenets of that religious sect, chief
among which was the duty of "gathering to Zion"

which meant our going to Utah. For fifteen
years we had feverishly been husbanding our
resources for that event, saving and skimping
to send, first, the oldest boy and girl, then
the next, and so on until at last we all would
reach that wonderful mecca of the faithful.

Although my father had been a sea-faring
man and subject to all the vicious tendencies of
that occupation; despite this, and the discourag-
ing influences and environment of the slums of
London in which we were brought up, we were
all piously obeying the teachings of that faith.
We did not drink nor swear nor use tobacco; we
did not use profane or boisterous language; we
kept ourselves clean and wholesome and were
faithful in our attendence at family prayers,
church services, and Sunday school; and we did
our share of street missionary work.

In pursuance of these duties my oldest
sister, seventeen, and my oldest brother, nine-
teen, who were to emigrate the following year,
attended a mid-week choir practice at St.
George's Hall near the Elephant and Castle.
This practice was directed by a Mr. George
Careless, whose name later became famous in
America as a composer and orchestral leader.
The method used was the "tonic-sol-fa" system.
So precocious was I and so persistent that it
was permitted me to accompany my elders to
rehearsals, where I was attentive and eager. I
quickly surprised the family by fluently voicing
the scale without any aid of instrument and in
carrying the airs and the words of the exercises
with a voice of considerable certainty.

Although this musical attainment may
seem a small item to the reader, I recall the
memory of it with a thrill of pride, not for itself, but that despite my tender age it led to
my ability to select the Magdalen quota for the
Queen's Choir, to participate in it, to infuse
spirit, pride, and enthusiasm in it, and to im-
part decorum to its behavior. My musical
ability led finally to recognition by the committee and then, more importantly, to my personal contact with Mr. Dickens.

CHAPTER VIII

Rehearsals for the Queen's Choir were in Exeter Hall, the largest auditorium in London. This huge hall, which I describe from uncorrected childhood memory, was circular or octagonal within and fully four hundred feet in diameter, with four walls without forming an enclosing square. In the center of the building an immense proscenium arch opened on to a stage a hundred feet deep, including a wide apron which extended over the orchestra pit. On either side of this arch were the banks of pipes of the largest pipe organ, at that time, in the world. The orchestra pit accomodated five hundred performers. The parquet seats rose steeply back to a very large foyer and above, extending back three hundred feet, were four immense galleries which climbed still more steeply to what seemed illimitable heights. It seated more than twenty thousand. The commission occupied the apron of the stage, behind which, rising bank over bank, were the seats of privileged spectators, while at either end of the apron were the boxes of royalty and the nobility.

Outside the circular or octagonal walls but within the square building were all kinds of booths, concessions, ticket offices, and wide winding stairs, for this was long before the era

of lifts.   It was a long arduous journey to reach
the topmost gallery.   The whole was brilliantly
(but for the topmost galleries) lighted with gas-
light.

At Exeter Hall at two o'clock every Saturday afternoon we twenty-five thousand gathered
for rehearsal.   Prior to the first rehearsal,
the Magdalen School quota assembled with all
the school's students and each choir quota member made a concerted and solemn vow that, "For
three months and until after the rehearsal," he
would be "decorous, faithful, loyal, patriotic,
and obedient" and especially that he would "not
fight nor incite to violence in public."   This
pledge was renewed in the presence of the school
assembly every Friday afternoon.   A refusal,
even a hesitation, to take this pledge forfeited
what had now come to be regarded as a supreme
honor; to lose this honor was a deep disgrace.

This plan of influencing the conduct of
the boys by an oral pledge was concocted and
put into effect by me myself as monitor of my
own school, little dreaming of an influence upon
the whole choir ensemble; but the plan was
watched and commented upon by other schools,
and evidently approved for before long it was
generally adopted.   This was two months before
I first met Mr. Dickens.

It was required that the master of each
school, or an accredited representative, should
accompany his own quota to the rehearsals as
guardian and to assist in the police regulations.
The guardians and the police were spaced throughout the assembly.   The members reported to

their masters at designated places before two
o'clock and after dismissal.

The voices were separated: the shrill,
strident, and high-tenor to the sporano class,
the mezzo and mellifluous to the alto and tenor,
and the sonorous and deep to the bass; but all
were child voices.

The work of the choir consisted princi-
pally in rendition of national and patriotic airs,
both our own and those of allied nations--for
this internationality was the prime purpose of
the thing--and these were interspersed with descriptive songs and roundelays and the like.   I
still remember the air and the words of many
of these songs.   A sample of the martial songs
is:

Forward, aye, forward, press shoulder to
shoulder,
In peace we're content but prepared for war;
Onward, aye, onward, each step growing
bolder,
We'll strive for our honor and peace ever-
more.
Here, all united, each comrade a brother,
The faith we profess in our deeds shall be
seen.
Heart and hand joining, we are sworn to
each other,
To fight and to die for our home and our
Queen.   Hurrah!

And this was a descriptive song:

Come, see our oars with feathered spray
Sparkle in the beam of day.
In a little boat we glide,
Swiftly o'er the silent tide;
Swiftly o'er the silent tide.

From yonder low and rocky shore
The warrior hermit to restore,   (repeat)
  While sweet the morning breezes blow
  While thus in measured time we row,
We row, we row, in measured time we
  row,
We row, we row, we row, we row, we
  row.

And this a sample of our roundelays:

A boat, a boat, haste to the ferry,
And we'll go over and be merry;
To laugh and quaff and drink good sherry

The twenty-five thousand of us were
taught also to produce in harmony certain sound
effects, by humming or scratching the backs of
our books for example, and there were some
mechanical effects for producing the booming of
thunder and of cannon and so forth.

CHAPTER IX

One Saturday in March, after more than
a month of rehearsals, for some reason or for
no reason at all unless it were fate, I started
out for Exeter Hall too early and arrived at the
last street corner before the Hall exactly at
12:30.   Mother always dressed me for this
affair in the best I had.   I was washed and
polished, hair-oiled and brushed, with cleaned
clothes, a shoe-shine, and a huge red kerchief
with a wide, flaming bow at my throat.   My
clothes were lovingly if not artistically fashioned
from the left-behinds of my elders.   I particularly remember my little fuzzy pea jacket.   It
had been made over from the material of a
former fustian sea coat of Daddy's that had seen
more years of service than I had seen of life.
It had nice little side pockets, as of course a
pea jacket must have, and I was very proud of
it.   On this day, in one of these pockets reposed a half-penny coin of the realm.   Knowing
London as few grown-ups did, I knew I was
running a risk to appear dressed in my best
with loose money in my pocket except that it
was mid-day and in a swell neighborhood, and
I was protecting my ha'penny with a tight clutch.

I am sure of the exact time I came to
that corner, for always at that instant, on every

66

street corner in all London, springing up through
the pavement, dropping from the clouds, resolv-
ing out the fog, Dickens' newsboys arrived like
miracles, shouting, "'ere's ya ha'penny edition,"
" 'ere's ya <u>Oliver Twist!</u> " " 'ere y'are," " 'ere
y'are," " 'ere's ya Dickens' <u>Oliver Twist,</u> on'y
a ha'pence!"

And for a half hour, Oliver Twist had
possession of all four corners everywhere and
then as mysteriously disappeared. The regular
newsboys who then appeared saw to it.

Therefore, one second after 12:30 that
little pocket in my pea jacket which had so
zealously protected a ha'penny was then protecting my latest chapter of <u>Oliver Twist.</u> This
was a second or third popular edition of that
gruesome and fascinating story: a single sheet,
folded once, usually containing one chapter on
the four pages. On the front page simply the
title appeared, except that in the upper left-
hand corner was a Charles Dickens portrait the
size of a penny and in the other corner, the
words "Ha'penny Edition." I had read the story
before and because of my retentive memory I
knew it almost by heart.

With Oliver Twist, then, and his creator,
was I preoccupied when, shopping done and
money all spent, I mounted the thirty-four steps
(I always counted them) of Exeter Hall. I knew
I was much too early. No one else was approaching the front door. Entering, I started
up the first flight of stairs--seventeen of them
to the first landing--pulling myself up, as boys
always do, by the baluster rail which was wide

and flat and smooth. As I did so I speculated
on the wonderful chance I had of belly-gutting
down that rail head first, ending with a hand-
spring on the floor below. There was no one
in sight. I knew I could do it.

      But, on the wall facing me (the stairs
turned right and left from this landing) there
was a very large portrait of a man standing in
the attitude of a statesman, right hand up-lifted
with digit extended (doing business as an orator
I suppose). It was Mr. Dickens. I had seen
the picture before but always when in an ascending crowd in which I could not stop. Now, all
alone, with one foot on the landing and the other
two steps below, my elbow resting on the rail,
my chin in cupped hand, I gazed and gazed and
dreamed for quite a while. I saw Little Nell
at Mrs. Jarley's wax works and Poor Jo sweeping his crossing and Little Em'ly at her boat
house home and Little Dorrit trailing Maggie
over London Bridge and then Bill Sykes and
Nancy and then I came to and turned to my proposed athletic stunt on the baluster rail. First,
I peered back apprehensively to see if the coast
were clear--horrors! there was a gentleman
coming up, pulling himself up, pulling on that
very rail as I had done, following in my very
wake; a man in a black, long-tailed coat with
a tall hat and gloves; whew! what a close
shave! I dissembled interest again, guiltily, in
the picture, hoping my improper intentions with
the baluster rail had not been divined. On and
on and on came the man and stopped by my side.
An arm stole over my shoulder--my heart missed
a beat--and then a gentle voice in a cheery tone
said,

"Well, my boy, what do you think of it?"

Relieved of my momentary fear, I looked
up and instantly recognized Mr. Dickens.
Dickens, my idol, here! in contact with me--
his arm around me--speaking to me! Now I
had no fear. I don't believe any boy ever had
any fear of Dickens, no precocious boy at any
rate. His question seemed so friendly.

Quickly I answered, looking from him to
the picture, "It's a jolly good picture of you,
sir," and then, in the same breath, I added,
"an'--an' I know the chimney that Bill Sykes
hung from!"

So far as Mr. Dickens might view it,
this was as irrelevant to his question as could
possibly be; but not so to me. Here was I,
one of a body of which he was the head. He
had always had my adoration. I had read
Oliver Twist and so was familiar with Bill Sykes
and his haunts; I had just spent my last ha'penny
on him. The only possession I had on me was
all about Bill Sykes--I still had my fingers on
him in my pocket. I had visualized him as I
gazed on the picture of the man who knew him
best, who had created him into flesh and blood
so that he could be hanged.

This reply to his question evidently
startled Mr. Dickens for he now squared himself toward me, stopped and grasped my
shoulders and exclaimed,

"Wha, you what? You know the chimney
that Bill Sykes hung from?

Then, apparently recovering himself he said, "That's queer, very queer, why, how could you--why--do you know?" Very imperatively he added, "where did you say it was, boy?"

I had not as yet said, as he knew I had not, but it was his way, as I afterwards learned, of drawing forth the mind of another. So with hands and tongue I proceeded.

"Sir, you know where Greyhound bridge is?" inquiringly, but certain of course that he ought to know.

He hesitated a bit as though recalling the fact. "Ya-es, Yes."

"Well sir, you know the mill-race that runs under it to the river down by the old mill?"

"Um-er, Ya-es." His conscience must have pricked him a little here even though the duplicity seemed necessary.

"Well, sir, you know the big red building on the other side of the water about half way down, the one with no windows in it and nothing but one big chimney on top? Well sir, that's it!"

"Well! Well!" said Mr. Dickens, "that's wonderful of you to find that chimney. You know, I had almost forgotten where it was myself. What is your name, Sonny?"

I told him. Proud.

"Oh! Billy, eh? And what school?"
Mr. Dickens of course took it for granted because of time and place that I was of the choir.

"Magdalen Ragged School, sir," I replied importantly, for had I not reason to be proud of that school's quota?

"And who is your master, Billy?"

"Mr. Harding, sir," and then to show that I approved of Mr. Harding, I added, "he's a proper man, sir."

"Oh, oh, well then, Billy, if he's such a proper man, you tell him when he comes that Mr. Dickens sends his compliments and wishes him to bring Billy down to the stage after this rehearsal."

Many people were now approaching the stairs and Mr. Dickens with a jolly tap on my head turned to the left and continued up leaving Billy dazed and gaping after him until he disappeared and then at the portrait as though it somehow embodied the real man who had just left him, until the oncoming crowd forced him onward to the right.

CHAPTER X

One may be sure that I watched eagerly
for the master's arrival at our rendezvous and
that I delivered my message with bubbling joy;
and equally sure that Mr. Harding expanded in
stature and warmed with pleasure at the com-
pliment I brought him. But there was no time
then for details as we had to separate for our
severel positions for the rehearsal, so these
were reserved until afterwards. Singing over,
Mr. Harding led me by long and devious ways
to the stage and I told him of my wonderful
adventure.

At length we reached the wings of the
stage. The curtain was now down and in the
glamor and tinsel and the brilliant lights that
gleamed with romance, I first beheld my fairyland, my most fantastic dream. I was thrilled,
gorging on the delight of it. Only gradually did
its reality dawn upon me with some degree of
comprehension.

Of course, from our vantage point in the
elevated and distant gallery we had often looked
down to this scene. We had seen the twenty to
thirty black-coated, silk-hatted gentlemen,
aristocratic and titled, who represented royalty
and who were the choir commission, but we

had never dreamed of so close a contact with
them as I had now.   These same gentlemen were
now at close range, in groups conversing, di-
recting workman and attendents, and Mr. Dickens
sat at a table facing us as we entered.

He immediately approached us and taking
my hand from the master's led me to his table
whereupon by some means attracting the attention of the commission he announced gravely:

"Gentlemen!   Gentlemen!   I want to introduce to you the boy who has discovered the
chimney that Bill Sykes was hanged from."

Naturally, this brought as much vivid interest from the audience as it did from me who
until now had no intimation of Mr. Dickens' purpose with me.

Surprise, incredulity, amusement, and
curiosity were blended in their faces as my
rosy cheeks deepened and fearlessly my wonder-
eyes surveyed the group.

They bombarded me with questions intended to disparage my claim but without avail.
I was made to tell with much particularity the
exact place and how you got to it and how I knew
so positively (and at the latter I weakened a bit
in my certainty of the place by dividing my as-
surance between my sublime faith in my own
discovery and the exactness of following Mr.
Dickens' description of it).   I may have had
some slight timorousness when I first claimed
this discovery but certainly none after I had so
successfully withstood their inquisition.

The location of this tragic and historic
event having now been definitely and for all time
determined and my reputation as an archeolog-
ical expert firmly established, Mr. Dickens returned me to my escort, to whom he now kindly
spoke, and after asking us for my parents' address he turned away.

But I was not so flabbergasted by this
thrilling adventure as to forget to take advantage of the opportunity it afforded of investi-
gating the miracle of artificial scenery and I
easily pursuaded Mr. Harding to take me through
the wings and drops which the stage hands were
now manipulating here and from the lofts above,
and I touched the paint and spangle which seemed
to have lost a little luster since seen from
above, and we went on the apron of the stage
where I looked up, instead of down, at the vastness of the tiers of seats.   And there was nothing to tell me that ten years later I would be a
part of just such an enterprise.

Looking backward, I now see that this
was an epochal period of my career which
marked my subconscious determination both to
make myself fit for contact with beings hitherto
beyond my ken and consciously to avail myself
of whatever opportunity such contact opened for
me.

There came to me a story I had heard
my father tell to illumine a discourse in his
street preaching to the effect that when he was
twenty-nine years he came across in his reading
the axiom that "opportunity knocks but once at

your door; seize it and ride to prosperity," and
that this had made a deep impression upon his
mind.   Shortly afterwards he had occasion to
cross a large open field; as he had recently been
reading of the sudden rise to fame of a noted
personage who had reached thirty-three years,
in the middle of this field and far away from
human hearing, he heard himself exclaim, "what
opportunity will present itself to me when I am
thirty-three?"

Distinctly he heard a voice in answer
say, "when you are thirty-three the plan of sal-
vation will be presented to you; watch for it, and
be led by it to a haven of peace."

The sequel of this story is that at thirty-
three something did happen that was of more
importance than anything else, so far, in his
life, and that eventuated in his removal to
another nation where he did find a "haven of
peace" that continued until he died.

This story, without any thought of its
sequel, had an effect upon me equal to that of
my meeting with Mr. Dickens.   The two things
together, at my impressionable age, had much
to do with molding my life character, in the
course of which these pages will shed light.

On my way home, accompanied on this
occasion by Mr. Harding, the meaning and the
importance of this wonderful interview was
volubly discussed.   The schoolmaster was very
familiar with and greatly admired Dickens'
works and the public reforms in which he was

engaged, and perhaps he could visualize the advantages that might accrue to me and perhaps
to himself and to Magdalen, or that for which
Magdalen stood, by this acquaintance. The inquiry for my address indicated that there was
something more to come and he gave me some
careful instruction and caution that were intended
to prevent my ruining my opportunity or, as he
said it, from "spoiling my kettle of fish."

CHAPTER XI

All of this of course, I gleefully reported
at home, bringing wide speculation as to what
Mr. Dickens could possibly want with our address.   But the mystery was not long-lived. On
the following week, Monday morning to be exact
for it was wash-day with all that that means in
household economies and house-wives' trials,
Mr. Dickens actually called on my mother and
baby sister, all the others of us being either
at work or at school.

Now, to have made this call in the morning, I learned afterwards, Mr. Dickens must
have driven direct from his Gad's Hill home on
his way to his city office, which he could do
without going very much out of his way, but
which he ordinarily would not do as to continue
on through Lant Street, where he once lived, to
the Borough Road and then over London Bridge
would have been cleaner and more pleasant.
But, for the purpose of making this visit he
turned on Bermondsey street at Bermondsey
church and following the directions I had given
him he found Bell Court, our home, just where
I told him it was, between a bake-shop on the
right and the Lion Pub on the left.

He must have been sharp-eyed indeed or

his coachman must have been sharp-eyed to have
discovered Bell Court, for its entrance was an
economy of space. It was wide enough only for
a push cart, which was the usual form of conveyence to the interior and the minimum width
the law allowed.

Between the walls of the shops mentioned
was a vaulted passage and from Bermondsey
Street it showed as a deep cavernous arch above
which, neatly and freshly painted, was the in-
signia: "Bell Court," and under this in smaller
letters: 'No Thorofare." This was indeed the
only fresh looking thing in the neighborhood.
And there was a reason for this.

The court was at least a century old if
one may compute age by appearances. It had
during all this time been known as "Cat Alley"
and perhaps no more appropriate cognomen
fitted its condition during these decades. But
when our family moved into it from Bacon's
Yard this plebeian title for our new abode rather
grated upon our fastidious nerves so that Father,
with clever diplomacy, prevailed upon Mr. Bell,
the owner to whom we were to pay twelve shillings per month rent, to permit him, Father, to
paint out the dilapidated Cat Alley sign and substitute the more euphonious title of Bell Court.

Perhaps this newly thought-out title captured Mr. Bell's imagination but his consent
carried with it strict provisos that he, Bell,
was to bear none of the expense and was to in-
cur no responsibility with the authorities and
that the "paintee" must square himself with the
other tenants.

So, Mr. Dickens must have gone through
this vaulted passage and on his left had been a
door which because of its obscurity may not have
attracted his attention but which if noticed at
closed hours for pubs would yield to observation
a variety of curious things; and at such times
this dark defile would be found a busy, very
busy, but noiseless thoroughfare.

And on the right side he had passed a
doorway which was "sanctified" in that it was
used only on Sundays through which to carry in,
on our way to Sunday school and on our return
to carry out, our Sunday baked dinners.   At
this holy and richly effulgent shop of juicy appe-
tizing odors, the front, on Sundays was religiously shutterred.

Having passed these unremarkable but
important apertures, Mr. Dickens had entered
the court proper, which he found fifteen feet
wide with an open drain running through the
center, swirling with wash-day suds probably
at that moment.   Then he had seen six separate three-story homes in side-by-side buildings with steep steps leading from each story
to the next room above, each having one window,
and each home, one door; these were much like
three soap boxes reached by ladders one above
the other about twelve feet square.   The flagged
floor of the court was littered with--well,
mostly with babies and with the innumerable
things that babies use and from wall to wall, at
the height of the second story, ran a net-work
of clotheslines upon which the abluted products
of the tubs were then appearing.   If, as one of
Lincoln's axioms has it, "you show me a back-

yard and I will show you the kind of people that
own it," then Mr. Dickens, with his powers of
observation, knew exactly what we were, indi-
vidually and collectively.

        And onward he picked his way between
gaping women washing and sprawling babies,
keeping to the left, to the end of the court and
to a high, brick wall surmounted with a still
higher iron fence, the wall and the fence ac-
counting for the "no   thorofare"   sign, and
perhaps he knew, for he had very good reasons
for knowing this neighborhood, that on the other
side of this wall was Christie's Hat Works,
Ltd., the largest hat works in the world. I
have personally conducted you, the readers,
along with Mr. Dickens, into this court and
along this wall to house No. 6, but here before
going in I wish competent witnesses among you
to stay to verify the remainder of the outdoor
portion of this scene.

        A sudsy wash-bench with a baby girl, an
abrupt shadow, a quick upward glance gets a
startled exclamation from a woman stopped busy
at a tub. Oh! I beg your English pardon! and
the woman beholds a silk-hatted man, a frock-
coated man, a gentleman, evidently; and the
gentleman beholds a clear complexion with ruddy
cheeks, surely blushing, large violet-blue eyes,
surely amazed, golden-brown, cared-for hair
in a net, a well-knit, substantial figure completely covered with an ample apron, shapely
hands, red and rough, and heavily booted feet:
my mother. Embarassed, she drops a pretty
old-fashioned courtesy and gazes inquiringly.

Mr. Dickens visits No. 6 Bell Court (pen-sketch by the author)

The court, which has from each tub and from each window and from each door taken in this invasion, now cautiously edges as near as decency permits to a point of vantage. Determining whether or not it approves.

After you have taken in all of this, noticing the gentleman's all-absorbing gaze, you hear Mr. Dickens say, gravely and with a knowing nod of the head:

"You are certainly the mother of little Billy."

But, if you had searched his eye and knew him, you would have seen homage for what else he saw, pity for what he realized, and humor for what surrounded him. But this remark, which also implied a question, has the effect of frightening the woman, because, as she afterwards told us, she did not immediately associate the gentleman with Mr. Dickens and so was alarmed for Billy who must certainly be in some sort of a "pickle," as she put it. ("Piratin' in the streets and got runn'd over, did 'e?")

The court and you witnesses now see an agonized face and imploring hands and quick cry, "What 'a 'e doon? What be the matter wi' 'un?" It takes some quick work on the part of the gentleman to introduce himself and then to reassure the woman by leading her into the house, thus shutting out both court and witnesses. (" 'E cood a knocked me doon wi' a feether so he cood.")

The interview must have been a long one,
judging by the time it took her to relate it later
for after her fright and when she was composed
again, she was questioned much about family
history, the occupation of each member of us
and how in the world she managed to keep such
an immaculate home on so small an income and
in such an environment (And oh! I would like
for you to have heard that.)

Then Billy was overhauled and, bless
her, how she did omit much that she knew and
much more that was worse that she didn't know
and much that she knew that Billy didn't know;
and 'ow she 'ad 'ad 'im in the Bay of Naples
on the sloop "Three Sisters" because the Wessel was took there, libelled, and couldn't leave
and 'ow 'er man the skipper wanted 'er to go
ashore to 'ave 'er baby, and 'ow she wouldn't
'ave anything to do with them furriners, and 'ow
at last 'er 'eavenly Father 'ad sent 'er a Irish
nurse, and 'ow it 'ad all turned out right arter
all except that she found out that the nurse was
a Catholic and not a Christian at all, and 'ow
at last the wessel was cleared and she got 'ome,
but never, never would she wentur aboard a
wessel again and 'ow glad she was that she 'ad
coaxed 'er 'usband to give up the sea and 'ow 'e
was a landsman now and a engineer in Bacon's
Tan Yards.

She sorrowfully admitted Billy's piratin'
'abits, but thank God 'e 'ad now left school as
'ed boy and was safe now as lather boy in a
ha'penny barber shop under a good, kind master.
(Poor, darling Mother; if she had only known
what a dreadful life and what a frightful tempta-

tion this occupation implied.)

Learning that I had Wednesdays off, for
I had to work on Sundays, Mr. Dickens asked
permission to take me with some other boys on
a picnic. Getting a rapturous consent to this
(Mother said Billy is such a industrious boy
and he works too 'ard) he instructed Mother
that on the following Wednesday week, that being
some sort of a holiday, Ash Wednesday I think,
I must meet him at nine o'clock at the Boar's
Head, a well known coach rendezvous where he
would pick me up for the picnic.

There was much more than this at that
interview, for scraps of it came pitching out
as it was remembered for some time afterward,
from Mother to the family and from Mr. Dickens
to me. One item later remembered by Mother:
evidently he was not content with "pumping" my
mother regarding her own affairs but had asked
her something regarding her neighbors to which
she had replied that she didn't know and on
second thought she had naively said:

"Our religion teaches us to mind our own
business and I do and so I don't know anything
about my neighbors and don't want to. "

Of course, Dickens, being a professional
reporter, would not suppose this answer had any
personal application, nor indeed was there any
intended. He may have hoped however that Billy
was not so thoroughly absorbed with that tenet,
since if he were he wouldn't be much use to him
as a coach.

(I have often thought that following my
declaration on the stairs and subsequently on
the stage at Exeter Hall and his quickly following visit to our home, that he had tentatively
formed the intention of singling me out from
among his boys and that what he had learned
on that visit had determined him on this course.)

After Mr. Dickens had gone the neighbors
were good enough to get the information over to
us that the coachman, evidently apprehensive,
had himself perilled the Bell Court passage
several times, that he had trailed his master's
footsteps to our door and had listened there,
and that the voices he heard therein had comforted him and he had returned to his waiting
coach. And Mother was good enough to get it
over to the neighbors that nothing had really
'appened to Billy but that she was just took
sudden loike, that was all.

CHAPTER XII

The intervening ten days leading to the
joyful Wednesday of the picnic galloped one
after another as usual, but anticipation led
Billy's mind far astray and to him the days
passed like magic. There was so much of the
picnic to speculate about. Where was it to be?
What was it for? Why was he invited? What
figure would he cut in the party? Oh! it was
all a mass of wonder and there was no one to
question. Many a slip the lather brush made
that week and many a cuff he got for it.

At home on the eve of that Wednesday
all hands sat up waiting for Billy's late arrival.
Mother was excited over it; Father, too, but
somehow suspiciously; brothers and sisters, too,
pleased but envious. All united to prepare for
it, each separately planning a surprise for it.
Finally Billy came, weary but elated. Forthwith and without waiting for him to finish supper,
came a pretty new striped shirt with wide, turn-
down collar (sister); forthwith came a beautiful
jockey cap with a crown in seven segments,
each of a different color, and with a wide pointed
peak (and Billy found it hard to swallow a mouth-
ful so that he could kiss his mother for it);
forthwith came a wonderful, white, ivory peg-
top that brother had turned (of which more later).

And his clothes were all cleaned and brushed
and laid out, and as all hands would be off to
work in the morning before his time for start-
ing, final instructions and mother's respects
and all their respects to Mr. Dickens were com-
mitted to him before retiring.

Well: daylight came, glory be! with no
note of postponement or abandonment; it was
not raining; in fact, it was a brilliant day for
London and there was nothing ominous impending.
Despite the instructions from Mr. Dickens that
I was to travel light, that all would be provided,
Mother stuck an apple in one pocket and a cooky
in another, "just to make sure," she said and
these together with things I myself had thought
of (including the ivory peg-top) made travel
heavy after all. It was thought prudent that the
jocky cap might be concealed while going through
the court, and then I was off on time to the
Boar's Head on the corner of Bermondsey New
Road and Old Kent Road.

Sure enough and near enough to nine
o'clock, up pranced four beautiful and gayly
caparisoned horses, and in rolled the freshest
painted and emblazoned coach you ever set your
eyes on; not a common hackney, mind you, nor
a regular omnibus, but the very coach that Mr.
Pickwick used to ride all over England in. It
was loaded inside and out with boys. Mr. Dickens
was partly inside and partly out for his head
was out of a window, evidently on the lookout
for me.

"Hullo, there," in the cheeriest voice in

the world called he.

"Good morning, Mr. Dickens" said I
bowing respectfully and doffing the jocky cap.
But from then on, I'm sure I quite forgot all
my mother's other instructions in etiquette.

"Climb in, Billy," and in I climbed, to
a seat beside Mr. Dickens who announced me
to the boys within ("this is Billy, boys") quite
as though I were a new specimen of boy, and
then, putting his head out of the window, he
announced me to the boys on top ("this is Billy,
boys") and then said to everyone, "now, we're
all here." Sufficient introduction, certainly, to
a jumble of boys of ten to thirteen years and
more than they had received, who had all been
picked up in a bunch at London Bridge and Mr.
Dickens later at St. George's Church.

Now this pick-up happened just within the
immense gates of the acre-square, cobble-paved
yard of the Boar's Head which was one of the
most prominent tourist inns of London. Quaint
old buildings surrounded the court on three
sides with a high-brick, spiked-top wall com-
pleting the enclosure. A wide and high-arched
driveway went under the inn to spacious stables
behind, where hundreds of big coach horses and
as many more of high-bred carriage horses
were stabled. Here, also, were all sorts of
vehicles in all stages of decrepitude; and there
were all kinds of shops there: smithy, shoeing,
woodworking, painting, and others all for the
purpose of getting these cripples back on their
wheels again.

The inn itself was the chief booking office
for all southern England with departures daily,
scores of them, and scores more at night. They
ran to Dover and Deal by way of Canterbury;
to the Channel Boats for France and Belgium;
to Faversham by way of Maidstone; to Brighton
and other south coast resorts; also to Portsmouth and Southhampton ports; and along all
routes to Salisbury, Dorchester and Exeter and
to Eaton, Oxford and other up-river college
towns past Windsor and Reading and everywhere
between.

Coaches swept into the court every few
minutes with sleepy passengers, tired horses,
and thirsty drivers; and others, just as often,
swept out with rested, prancing horses, cracks
of whips, and freshly washed out throats of
fresh drivers. There was much champing of
bits, stamping of hoofs, hurrying of hostlers,
hurrying footmen, hurrying porters, hurrying
clerks, buglers, and luggagemen. Passengers
getting off called for porters; passengers getting
on stowed their luggage: much yelling, many
orders, impatience, and confusion but all good-
natured.

"Well! What are we waiting for, eh?
Ah! We're off, we're off! Hip! Hip!"

"Tally-ho--o-o-o," sounded the bugler
and out we went and off we went, and me in
such a daze I hardly knew if I were sitting or
standing or cartwheeling: beside the real Dickens,
the creator of the jolly Pickwick crowd, rapturously riding with him in the same kind of
old coach, in the same old jolly way. Ah! If

there are any among you who have missed this
sort of treat, get to it quickly, for life is a
blank until you have enjoyed this cheeriest, most
informative, most exhilarating, and most entertaining way of viewing Merry Old England, with
its thousands of old nooks and corners.

"We're off for Windsor Park, boys!"
shouted our host, and then to the driver through
the pilot hole: "Windsor Park, Tony." Tony!
Is it possible? Tony! Tony Veller? The immortal Tony? Or is it only the departed shade
of Tony repatriated to earth for this special
occasion?

"Hurrah! Hurrah!" we shout. For this
is the first moment we have known of our destination. Although Windsor is but a few hours
from the city I doubt if any of us boys had ever
been there or had ever expected to go there,
never, at least, so auspiciously!

We surely were a random group. I
never knew how Mr. Dickens had collected us;
it is certain we were all poor boys. Only two
others I feel sure, the brothers William and
Alfred Keene (whom I met several times afterwards), were, with myself, what he called
"my boys." He doubtless had his reasons for
including us with the others, or, for including
the others with us.

Because of the hubbub and un-bottled enthusiasm during the outward journey there was
not much chance for conversation and yet in one
way and another during the day he did quiz us a
good deal and perhaps drew from us some useful

information. At least he took a lot of animation
from us and got it into himself, for he was the
jolliest among us, quite like a kid and not a bit
impatient over any of our pranks.

Mr. Dickens was dressed this day in
tweeds with knickers and leggings and a tweed
Scottish cap. He carried a stout stick and had
thick gloves but didn't wear them. Oh! He
was quite a different looking person and a different acting person from the dignified, black-
coated, silk-hatted Mr. Dickens, Chairman of
the Queen's Choir Commission to whom I first
spoke a fortnight before. He had stepped out of
that picture and now into a coaching picture he
himself had created with himself and us, his
characters. I wonder did Pickwick and his
glorious hosts accompany us.

In remembering this incident, I am led
to wonder at the motive prompting Mr. Dickens
for this momentary relaxing from his accustomed
austerity. Was it simply a desire to give a
treat, to raise the spirits of a lot of poor boys?
Was it a hunger to be a boy himself again? Or
was it just the necessity of relaxing, of shaking
off the cares that beset him and the people that
besieged him? I feel sure that no other account
of this outing exists; who knows, if there is such
a thing as the soul of the departed guiding the
actions of mortals below, but that his amending
soul is prompting now the chronicling of this unusual red-letter-day in the midst of his haras-
sing career.

CHAPTER XIII

So, with the most famous driver in the
world holding the ribbons, away we go, pell-
mell down the oldest road in England. Sun a-
shining as if never obscured; whip cracking to
the prancing leaders. Through the smoke we
went with never a green thing in sight, then
out of it past the Parliament Houses through St.
James with its bright greens and budding flowers
with Westminster Abbey off to the right, through
the Mall and past Buckingham Palace, then Hyde
Park and the Serpentine seen in the distance
across the river, past market gardens with their
serried rows of greens and browns, along fresh
green hawthorn hedges with white and Magenta
blooms, and then out among the open fields with
brilliant butterflies swarming overhead and spring
birds trilling their welcome to us. Then in
sight came pastures and parks with noble trees,
mansions, and handsome residences. Up each
long hill with labor, and down a-galloping; over
the bridges a-rattling; through the fords a-
splashing. People watched and waved who little
guessed that the great Charles Dickens captained
the coach. On board, boys climbed from below
to the roof; boys tumbled from roof to below.
All above telling Tony this and that, just as
though he did not already know everything (being
immortal), all below quizzing Mr. Dickens for

this and that.   We pranced through populous
Kingston with its streets so spic and span,
through pretty villages with orchards and hopeful
gardens, past colleges, seminaries, young ladies'
schools, naval academies, nunneries, and hospi-
tals.   Through the dells and woods and green-
swards we swooped, and at last, but all too
quickly, we were in the deep, shady, hedgerow
bordered drive that told us we were within
Windsor.

It was clear to us that we were nearing
the entrance to the park, for now, on either side
of the broad thoroughfare and between hawthorn
hedges, were licensed concessions of certain
secluded kinds.   There were bridle paths amid
pretty shrubbery and wide spreading trees on
either side of the river which was flanked with
old-fashioned inns and road houses that stretched
to Oxford and beyond.   White shady lanes ran
this way and that, with beautiful galloping horses
and gallant riders.   There must have been
royalty and nobility among these, of course.
There were many liveried lackeys and grooms.

The concessions offered donkeys and Shetland ponies for hire, and elephants and dromo-
daries and camels and ostriches for riding.
Red-coated soldiers stood on duty; there was
cleanliness and neatness and order and such decorum as to hush and induce good behavior.
There were pretty nurses and staid governesses
and white-capped maids for richly dressed little
boys and girls, who to us were princes and
princesses.

The river could be seen in vistas between

the trees and on this were gay little boats with
gayly dressed young ladies and college-dressed
swains, sailing or rowing. Past all these we
drove, quiet, and between immense stone pillars
and high spiked gates we paused. There was
now some arrangement between our major-domo
and the gold-braided guards, and then in we drive
with a flourish and on to a grassy sward and
near to a quaint old stable and a village of empty
dog kennels. It is high noon. We are in Windsor Park. Hurrah! Hurrah!

     Out we pour and down we climb, some
helping Tony with the horses to the stables for
their feed, some helping with the unpacking of
the picnic hampers for our feed and the spreading of it supervised by Mr. Dickens, and oh!
how hungry we were.

     In a few minutes we were all assembled
again. There came strict orders to lunch at
our leisure, then, after the lunch to pack up
and stow the remains by one o'clock. Then we
might explore wherever we would within the park
but were to be sure to be back to the coach by
two o'clock.

     "And then," said Mr. Dickens, with an
air of mystery, "if you behave and only for
such as do behave there is to be another treat."

     The nature of this treat he did not divulge.
This was a pretty good scheme, of course, to keep
us reasonable within bounds.

     From sixty years of memory I can still
picture that beautiful old park, which through so

many centuries has been Royal Domain, which
has been played in by royal children, courted in
by princes and princesses, walked and riden in
by kings and queens, hunted in by courtiers and
gallants, plotted in by assassins and conspirators, and which has been the scene of many a
ballad, many a play, and many a good book of
romance and history.   It contains in its three
square miles big old oaks and elms and beeches
of enormous spread that could tell of many a
love proved or made a tragedy beneath their um-
brageous foliage since the time of Cardinal Wol-
sey.   It all belonged to the Crown and was not
open to the public except by special permission
from the Royal Chamberlain, which Mr. Dickens
must have previously secured.

As soon as the picnic was spread and the
boys assembled again and ready for it, Mr.
Dickens placed us under the charge of Tony and
went away.   Perhaps picnic feeding did not
agree with him but he did not pain us by saying
so.   Perhaps he wanted a surcease of us for a
rest but he did not say this either.   Perhaps he
really did have business elsewhere, or he needed an afternoon nap.   At any rate he did go
away and he did not return until three o'clock.

During the picnic meal I had continually
cast longing eyes through the visitas of sunlight
and shade of that grand old wood of the park.
I had a sensation of escaping from some condition of thraldom that oppressed me into a domain
of light and liberty and freedom that belonged to
me.   I evaded the chores after eating.   I anticipated one o'clock a bit.   I shed my jacket,
shoes, and cap and minutes sooner than the

others were ready I made off like an elf into
the forest and hardly saw them again during
that hour. I ran, I catapaulted into cartwheels
and somersaults, I climbed, I leaped into trees,
I cavorted into the gloom and exalted in the
sunlight, all in the most exuberant of spirits.
I felt free, free, as I had never felt before.

The sun beat down in glee. I yelled and
whistled and sweated and panted. I reached a
boundary hedge of heliotrope, into which I
smothered my face and arms; bounding away in
another direction, I came to a large open space.
Halting here to wipe off my sweating face and
eyes, I beheld an opening which made a vista
clear through the forest of big trees. At its
end was what I knew must be Old Windsor
Castle. It has never had a better setting than
that in which I first viewed it. The outlines of
its upper portion, with its big central tower, its
many turrets and its castellated walls, stood out
as clear-cut as a cameo (and still does in my
memory), although it was fully three miles distant and elevated on a considerable eminence.
I gazed in rapture through the clear and radiant
atmosphere as at a heavenly vision and thoughts
of boundless opportunities raced through my
mind. I aged in that one hour. My old content
that everything was right was gone forever. I
knew I was in a world of my own making and
my future depended upon myself.

These reflections over, I thought it
strange that I should be all alone and feared I
had overstepped the hour. Just then there came
the bugle call from the gates: our signal for assembly. In a few minutes I was trundling into

camp in cartwheels, to the evident amazement
of Tony and the boys, and thereby revealed to
them my profession. I learned to my surprise
that none of the other boys had been farther a-
field than the neighboring blackberry bushes,
on which they had glutted in spite of their already
full stomachs. For this they later paid a painful
penalty. I had made at least three miles, had
witnessed a thousand wonders in the loveliness
of nature in her happiest moods, and I had had
a comprehensive and picturesque, though re-
mote, view of a medieval castle, which I had
no dream of seeing nearer, and I had had a
vision of the wide, wide world, which I might
reach after and attain.

And now that I have related this incident,
I wonder again--as I have ever wondered--why
these boys, all of them, had failed in finding
for themselves the glory of what I had partaken
of so rapturously and which was as clearly within their reach as in mine. I mention it here
because it afterwards made the subject of a useful conversation with my patron. My outbreak
of athletics on this occasion also reached his
ears, which made not only another topic for conversation, but gave another illustration, of which
he received many at every convenient but private
opportunity, of my agility. Through just such
conversations as this about my singular exploration of the park, Mr. Dickens learned all about
my dangerous and disgraceful slum and alley
life, my street tumbling, my underworld experiences, my small achievements, and my be-
liefs. And he had heard of, and he had applaud-
ed, my hopes and aspirations for a much different and more exalted career.

Then, at three, with all our entertainment programs completed, including exhilarating
rides out onto the highway on the animals we
saw at the entrance; with the horses fed,
watered, and ready to hitch up, pawing and
champing to be off; everything packed up and
all hands accounted for; Mr. Dickens back and
a favorable report from Tony as to our behavior; our mentor amazed us, after a little
humorous preamble, by announcing with a
flourish, "boys, we're going to the castle!"

My! How we caught our breath and how
we yelled in chant: "hurrah! hurrah! We all
love Mr. Dickens because he's been so good!"
My pleasure at this wonderful announcement may
easily be conceived, after my moving vision of
the castle earlier.

And now we may add another "perhaps"
to the speculation about Mr. Dickens' picnic
absence--perhaps he had been arranging for this
very treat and had already gone on one of his
long, striding walks to Windsor Castle and back
to get it.

CHAPTER XIV

It was very near time to start to Windsor Castle but an inspection taken of our condition showed us that we were scarcely fit for association with our host and certainly less for presentation at a Royal Court, what with our running, cartwheeling, sweating, and plunging into shrubbery and smearing ripe blackberry stains. It was decided that we must first wash up and get presentable.

Hard-by us was the horse-trough and pump. We were commanded to shed our jackets and "go to it." Mr. Dickens mounted Tony's box on the coach and stood in the attitude of a ring-master in the circus, the better to direct this work and, I feel sure, to get some fun out of it also. The usually provident mothers of us boys had this time been too trusting for we hadn't a towel nor a comb among us. But our phantom driver, doomed as he was to live with his coach and therefore ever equipped for all emergencies, produced a comb and two towels and some cakes of soap.

While we washed, Tony and Mr. Dickens called things out to us.

"Be loively, young uns; I carn't 'old

these 'ere 'osses furever."

Mr. Dickens yelled to Reddy because of his fiery hair, "Here, Reddy, you pump, you don't want a comb, you need a fire engine"; and to another, "Don't get into the trough, Harry, have some respect for the horses!"

At last, with bantering and exhortations, we were all within or on top of the coach again. Tony gathered his lines, poised his whip, and another merry prolonged "tally-ho" came from the bugler at the gates, bringing cheerful subdued echos from the forest and hills. The whip cracked and we were off again! This time for Windsor Castle.

Long before this the reserve between us boys had broken. We now knew each other by name or nickname. Two were the Keene brothers of whom I have spoken and who were now at Magdalen and whom I was to meet often again. Some were at grammar schools or primaries; some were orphans; some were newly discovered, others were well known to our host; but all were poor slum boys. Seemingly we had all of us recently taken on a determination to make something of ourselves for most of our talk was as to what we intended doing when we would be grown up. Now, alas, they and their names and their personalities are all, except the Keenes, forgotten memories.

The road to the castle is rather steep climbing at places, overcoming hundreds of feet

of elevation.   At first it parallels the highway
leading to the towns of Windsor and Eton, then,
leaving that road, it takes a short cut over a
ridge and, hugging the hillside, ascends the
steepest part of the south side of the hill, or
mountain as the natives call it.   The coach and
cargo make quite a load for such a drag but
our team doesn't mind it; the leaders had to
buckle into it a little harder, that's all.   It did
reduce our speed a bit and that was a good
thing for it reduced the pitching and the swaying
and gave us a chance we never again would have,
for a comprehensive view of at least six counties
and shires of England: Middlesex, Surrey, Buckingham, Hartford, Hampshire, and Berkshire.

The road which was mostly hillside but
broad and splendidly surfaced with crushed red
stone, was all curves and windings around the
mountain in its ascent which permitted a wide
view in all directions.   In the lovely river valley
the parks of lawn and flower gardens made a
pretty background for stately churches, colleges,
and abbeys which lined the river shores and the
edges of other streams that entered it.   Below
us, between the hill base and the Thames,
snuggled the pretty town of Windsor, made
memorable by many old romances and historical
tales.   Mr. Dickens pointed it out, telling us
that if we had read Shakespeare's The Merry
Wives of Windsor we could there in Windsor
easily fancy the homes of Mistress Ford and
Mistress Page and the pickle in which they put
the doughty Sir John Falstaff and see all the
jolly jokers of that comedy; and he bade us read
it.

He also pointed out Eton, the oldest college town in England, just across the river from
Windsor and in Berkshire with only an artistic
stone bridge between. He pointed out the distant
downs of these counties with the many cities and
villages thereon; and when we reached Lookout
Observatory at the top, we could see the spires
and minarettes and domes of ancient Oxford.
We could have had no better guide than Mr.
Dickens, nor a better story teller.

Time flew even if our coach did not. It
was four o'clock and now we were halted by a
wonderfully emblazoned officer of the Royal
Grenadiers. A salute and a conversation with
our host (who seemed to have been expected)
which included a lot of do's and don't's which had
to be observed from then on, and open came the
gates of a majestic portal and in we drove with
a dash that seemed to say "well, here we are!"
and out of the coach we poured, a little shy and
a little on our good behavior, impressed with
the splendor and massiveness of all around us.

Two Grenadiers of apparently lesser
rank, were assigned to us as guides. Orders
had been given them which included positively
the return of us by six o'clock. And then, in
orderly procession we proceeded, now without
Mr. Dickens who excused himself, and without
even Tony who had all he could attend to in order
to get ready for our return journey.

We were bidden to walk fast, pay attention, touch nothing, ask questions, yes, but
quietly, and not to talk to each other. We came
to big pillars with gates already open, with

mounted cannon and a red-coat soldier on either
side, looking very fierce, with muskets and
fixed bayonets.   Beyond the gates there was a
wide bridge spanning a deep ditch which, it was
explained, was a moat, dry now, but in former
times of danger, filled with water; that an-
ciently it had entirely encircled the castle but
was now filled up except under this bridge where
it was left as a spectacle.   The bridge ended at
a massive wall fully fifty feet in height which
stretched all around the grounds and in which
were turrets and loop-holes, with pointed cannon
and other red-coat watchmen parading here and
there the top.   In this wall was a heavy armored
gate, closed, but with smaller ones in the round
pillars at the sides which I learned were called
postern doors.   Through these we passed.   We
saw the heavy iron portcullis poised high up between the pillars looking like spiked gates turned
upside down.   Its purpose and operation was explained to us.   We crossed a wide open paved
space that followed the wall on the inside through
smaller gates in an iron fence and we were in
the grounds of the palace proper.   Now we were
hurried through lanes lined with statuary, mon-
uments with tablets commemorating this and
that, past old-fashioned sun dials and marble
seats, past marble fountains--now at rest--to
a noble marble entrance of what we were told
was the "north court. "

Here we were turned over to other
guides, in livery this time, and we were hurried
through corridors as wide as streets and permitted to view from just within their doorways
the ceremonial halls, the banquet halls, the
royal ballroom, and the throne room--the fur-

nishing of which and the portraits and pictures
and armory of which were heavily draped. Up
winding marble stairways with heavy balustrades
and lined with men-at-arms in ancient armor
we went, and through other wide halls for a
peep into the bedrooms of Anne Boleyn, Charles
the Second, Queen Elizabeth, our own good
Queen, and many others. We were shown the
chair that Sir Walter Raleigh sat in, the table
where such-and-such documents were signed and
from "the wery same ink pot and the wery same
pen too," and the desk of so-and-so. From
there we were taken to the royal kitchens, where
all within was also draped and from which even
the valuable tableware had been removed, except
samples of it.

And in less than a half hour we were
again turned over to our outer guides, the Grenadiers, for a further exploration of the grounds
and of the castle itself and also the immense
circular tower, ominous and sinister, that
stands in the middle between the north and south
courts. Here we were shown ancient dungeons,
heavily gated and barred. There were hints of
terrible torture chambers and secret executions
of traitors and conspirators, and of long im-
prisonments of noble persons who had stood in
the way of kings and queens. We were taken up
winding stairs of stone and shown council chambers and soldiers' and officers' quarters, and
on to the roof, where were more pointing cannon
and parapets for sharpshooters, and from which
we had a lovely view in every direction of the
countryside.

From this we were hurried to the greatest

thing of all, the maze.   It would never do to go
to Hampton Court without seeing the maze;
nearly everybody at home and abroad had heard
of it.   Most people, excepting the timorous, had
been in it.   Now, children, and especially girls,
came under the head of timorous certainly, but
Dickens' boys could not be so classified.   The
guards (who dearly liked to rub it into small
boys) mysteriously told us of the direful things
that had happened therein, always at "just this
time of day when the low setting sun cast long
goblin-like shadows and just when the keepers
were off duty" and how "it didn't seem right to
send children in there, knowing what they (the
guards) knew," and to add to this lugubriousness
a couple of navvies, digging nearby, were particularly solicitious about us.   One, climbing
out of this ditch, came over to us and looked
us over commiseratively.

"You bain't gooing into that ploice, be ya?"

"You bet ya," say we.

"Soi, Sergeant," says he, " 'ow erboot
that fella that went in a week agone yestereen
an' neever coomed oot?"

"Can't 'elp that; orders is to make 'em go.
There's 'unner's 'o 'em as don't coom oot. "

"Dang'd if I'd go in fer a hunnerd bob,"
whines the navvy, turning sorrowfully away.

"Now then kids, moike it loively, in ye
goes.   Hif ye're ain't back 'ere when the bell
tolls the second toime we'll send the blood 'ounds

in arter ye, that's what.   Git! "

    Most of us vanished with alacrity into
the maze. We were quickly separated, for no
two could agree, of course, as to which turning
to take. The solid block hedge of boxwood was
impenetrable to sight and unscalable to climb,
even without the warning signs not to attempt it
under severe penalty.

    We could hear each other, but this only
increased the confusion, since everyone's directions were misleading and exasperating. By
the tolling of the first bell, only two had reached
the goal, which was a circular court in the
center of the maze with a little glass house in
which to register one's name. As none were
out when the second bell tolled, in an instant
we heard the deep, drum-toned baying of the
bloodhounds. We heard them coming nearer,
baying and panting; closer, closer they came,
panting more fiercely. Now! They were on us!

    But, to our great relief they were the
keepers, who were certainly good mimics of
bloodhounds and who quickly accounted for all
of us on the outside. The two navvies seemed
much comforted by our reappearance. Dickens
too was there to receive us and laugh at us and
chaff us to hurry us to the coach. He first,
however, slipped a bit to each of the guards
with a word of thanks, receiving their respectful
salutes and their help in getting us loaded on.
Homeward bound on time: six o'clock.

    Oh! what a day! More things had hap-
pened in that one day than had ever happened

before to any kids like us in a lifetime.   There
was more to tell of what we had seen and done
than we could account for in a score of lifetimes.

With the horses refreshed, their noses
pointed homeward, we fairly flew down the road
we had toiled up only hours earlier.   We were
at the park gates again in no time but did not
stop.   The remains of the picnic food and a
hamper of pop was served out below and sent up
aloft.   It was only now that our patient host
could get a word in edgeways.   Even so, it
would have been a wonder if he made out anything
coherent from our excited replies to his questioning.   We found that while we had been climbing hills and stairs breathlessly and running in
the maze frantically and getting hungry and tired,
he had been resting, sleeping, in the coach,
where Tony had made him comfortable.

The satisfaction of this second meal now
quieted us down and at last gave him the floor.
He told us of his own first visit to the Royal
Court when he was a boy, but a bit older than
we; and that he had since been there with other
gentlemen on affairs of state by invitation of the
Queen, and that in these visits he had been able
to see much more than we did, because the Royal
residence which was formerly at Hampton Court
was now moved to the Isle of Wight and the
hunting, which was formerly in the Park, was
moved to Balmoral.   And he told us that the old
Court and its castle was now only a show place
for the public at certain seasons and occasions
and that was why we found so few soldiers there
and why things were covered up or moved away.
It being out of season, he had been obliged to

get a special permit for our visit; but he hoped
we would always treasure the memory of it.
He also said that this accounted for our not finding deer and antelope and elk and the Royal dog
kennels in the park, as we had expected, for all
of these were now moved to Scotland where there
was more room for game.

And he told us more about the Queen as
she appeared to him, but I think he intended to
convey to us only such impressions as befitted
childish ears and that would enhance our loyalty
toward her.   And he told us a lot more about
the new route we were taking and which led us
partly along the north side of the river.

"And now," he said, "since we have been
talking so much about our Queen, what do you
say to our stopping at the next bridge-end, and
getting out and singing " 'God save our gracious
Queen'?"

"Hurrah!" we chorused.

"And Billy will lead it," said he; "he
knows how."

So the word was passed up to the boys
above and to Tony on the box and in a few minutes we were all in a circle in the middle of the
road, capless, I, capless, in the middle, Dickens on the roadside, capless, and Tony on the
box, hatless.   And with a peal of patriotic fervor
such as was never heard on a bridge-end before,
that loyal old hymn went up and down the Thames,
and over and around the countryside, and back
and back again came the echoed refrains.

I think the standing there and the singing
produced the same thoughtful impression on the
other boys that it did on me.   For in that glorious holiday with the shade of Pickwick, we
had been given a view of merry England's most
historic highway with a traveller of experience
to guide us; a splendid picnic dinner; a wonderful
zoological excitement; a conducted view of a
Royal Palace; a baffling experience in the maze;
but above all a close contact with one of the
world's most adored story tellers.   And we had
found him a generous, light-hearted host who
had revealed to us a joyous character that few
in the world have.   We had been guests of a man
who loved the world, and especially its boys,
and knew how to make allowances for their environment, their lack of culture, and their inex-
perience; a man who had not preached Sunday-
school twaddle to us; who had permitted our
ebullient behavior yet had found chances for interesting instruction; who had used no harsh,
coarse, vulgar, or slang language himself yet
had not chided us for any such indiscretion. In
fact, Mr. Dickens was a democrat of democrats.
We might all then, gathered to sing, have resolved that we could and would emulate his
example.

The sun was sinking now, so while we
were halted the lamps were lit on the coach,
red to port and green to starboard, the tinkling
fog bells were hung on the leaders' hamebows,
the bugle was placed ready in case of fog, and
we were off again.   Our host then informed us
that we were traveling by a different route, for
variety and because it would leave him at a certain railway station.   But we were told that we

boys would all be taken to the Boar's Head because the coach and the shade of Tony Veller
belonged there.

He gave some of the boys instructions for
later use, and to me, his respects to my mother
with the word that he would call on her again
soon when he hoped Father also would be at
home.

And then he was off at the railway station. I think there were sobs in some of us at
this last minute but we managed to get out a
"hurrah! hurrah! we all love Mr. Dickens because he's been so good."

I wonder if he had a repressed sob.   I
like to think he had; and I am sure that he had
had his day of fun too.   I saw him many times
after this but never again in the same happy
care-free mood of that day, nor anything like it.

CHAPTER XV

To illustrate the deep feeling of respect and admiration amounting to love that Mr. Dickens' conduct toward me had inspired, I will relate an incident that has remained fresh in my memory, since it was "the fly in the ointment" that was to mar the perfection of that picnic day of bliss.

My brother Fred, fourteen, was a stationary engineer in a kid leather tannery, an expert mechanic at nine shillings a week. Adjoining his tannery was a turning shop for wood and bone. As Fred's engines furnished the power for this shop also, he had the run of it. Being mechanically skilled and super-industrious he took every spare moment from his engine to practice on the lathes until he had acquired considerable ability.

Finding one day, in the waste heap of this shop, a chunk that resembled bone, Fred had cleaned it up and decided that it lent itself to the turning of a peg-top. He resolved to try his hand on it, whereupon the supposed bone turned out to be pure ivory. With his utmost skill and with some assistance he fashioned it into a beautiful top. In making it he had no other thought than of keeping it for himself, but his generous

disposition, which I recall ran spasmodically,
induced him, just as the other prizes for gradu-
ating as head boy at Magdalen were coming to
me, to give this top to me as his contribution.

I was very, very proud of it and grateful
to Brother and as I said, made it a part of the
impedimenta to the picnic. There had been no
chance of course to spin it on the journey but it
had been passed around among the boys and perhaps had excited some envy among them. It had
been admired by Mr. Dickens and its history related to him as I have here set it down.

The peg-top had then reposed in the little
pocket of my pea jacket. When later I shed the
jacket, shoes, and cap for that gambol in the
forest, it was still in that pocket. When I returned, washed up, and donned the jacket, it
was gone. I was amazed and heartbroken and
excitedly hunted for it and made inquiries but to
no avail. All declared they had seen nothing of
it. Had I worn the coat to the woods I might
easily have supposed I had lost it there. But
it was certain it had disappeared in camp--in
the camp of my friends. Mr. Dickens had been
away; Tony had been busy at the stables (never
once did I suspect him); no visitors had been in
the camp. Who of the other boys could have
taken the top? Was someone teasing me? Had
someone stolen it?

I was in a dilemma. To make a stir
about it would cause a scene. It might cause
the boys to be searched and it would disgrace
someone if found; it would put a stigma on everyone if not found. What to do? To complain to

Mr. Dickens would spoil his pleasure and lessen
his confidence in all of us. And so, I resolved
on saying nothing and I pledged the boys to say
nothing more about it and at all events to keep
the matter from our host.

Now I was too young to have so resolved
from any good sport instinct, from any thought-
out effect it would have on that "additional treat"
that had been promised. I think that at the time
I was influenced only by my acquired affection
for Mr. Dickens and an instinctive wish to keep
from him any pain. So far as I knew he was
not aware of my loss and fortunately there was
enough excitement and distraction over other
matters that it did not bear heavily on my mind,
then; but I had a hard time on my return home
to account for my loss without incriminations--
especially to explain to the generous donor.

When Mr. Dickens left home that day of
the picnic I do not suppose that he informed anyone that he intended taking a lot of poor slum
boys on a picnic to Windsor Park. Since later
on I became a bit familiar with the regime of
his household, and using my analytical mind in
putting two and two and this and that together, I
am inclined to think that when he came down to
breakfast at seven o'clock that morning dressed
in his walking tweeds, he was probably quizzed
as to "what's up, gov'ner?" but in no very surprised way, for, having what we Americans call
a "hiking suit" (a word that is in no English
dictionary) we may suppose that he often used
it in the fond pursuit of cross-country walking.
It is known that he did this health-promoting

exercise whenever he got a chance, even walking
all the way from Gad's Hill to his office in the
city whenever he could get agreeable company.

I would say that he answered that morning question, "Oh, I'm going to run up river a
bit with some cronies of mine."

Which, you see, would be no deception,
even though cronies in this case, as the family
would view it, would be respectable gentlemen
of his own class.

It does seem certain that he must have
planned this "run up the river" at least a week
before, for he would have to book it at the
Boar's Head several days prior. This he could
conveniently do and probably did as his barouche
passed that hostelry whenever he drove to town.

But why might Mr. Dickens not have been
perfectly frank about what he planned doing that
day? My answer is that he knew very well that
the family did not wholly approve of his democratic leanings and especially of the course it
took toward plebeian acquaintances. The family
aspired to a more exalted sphere of society and
naturally wished the head of the house to pull it
up, not bear it down by low association. What
would the more exalted sphere think if they
knew he was taking a crowd of rag-a-muffin
mudlarks on an expensive journey in a fine coach
right into the sacred precincts of royalty itself?
Surely it would not be approved that his own
children associate with such pernicious scamps.

Of course, this belief of mine may be all

balderdash but it has taken a lifetime of reason-
ing about the nature of Mr. Dickens' family to
have reached this deduction.   It does not imply,
I hope, that there was or is any disrespect in
my mind toward an "estimable family" with aspirations.

It should be borne in mind that this day
off for healthful exercise was taken while Mr.
Dickens was in the midst of promotion work as
Chairman of the Queen's Choir Commission--
a world of detail for a man overwhelmed with
business of his own.   He was swamped at this
time with public reading engagements and de-
mands from his publishers.

CHAPTER XVI

So, several weeks passed during which
I lived over and over again the delights of that
one day; recounted to the family redundantly the
minutest particulars of it; speculated on the
reasons for it and the outcome of it; and spread
lather at the barber shop in dreamy abandon.
I waited impatiently for the next word from Mr.
Dickens.

At last it came, a note to Mother, asking
that I meet him at a well-known coffee house in
Fleet Street near Ludgate Hill (near his publish-
ing house, I think) on the following Wednesday
exactly at noon. On that day with great care I
was arrayed in my Sunday best, ready for the
city and much too early. Because of this, and
much to my joy, Mother proposed going with me
as far as the first recess of London Bridge from
the seat of which we could watch the traffic on
the river while the final do's and don't's were
impressed upon me.

No better opportunity will be afforded for
a description of this busy marine artery to the
packed millions of London's population. For
Mr. Dickens as a boy not only studied it from
the same granite seat that I was then seeing it
from, but he had known it under the same woe-

116

fully distressing conditions that I had known it
and he had used it in his happier later life in
all its phases for the expression of his characters.

To him, the river had been full of romance and tragedy and comedy as well. It
became so familiar to him that he thought and
dreamed and wrote in the idiom of it; pictured
and painted its denizens in the colors of it; conceived some of his strongest subjects from the
unique characters he found on it and I have no
doubt he had prowled its margins and deepest
haunts personally.

From our vantage point off to the right,
at the foot of Magdalen Alley, was Quilp's rotten
wharf and yard, from the warehouse of which
he stumbled in terror to his fatal exit, and where
Tom Scott, for whom I have a peculiar affinity,
practiced his sarcastic gymnastics. A mile beyond was the romantic yard of Captain Cuttle,
cluttered up with his lifelong accumulation of
figureheads. Immediately under us were the
dark arches of the bridge and the darker arches
under the wide approaches to the bridge. In
these slimy recesses lurked Fagin and his motley
crew at midnight and Bill Sykes planned his
burglarous forays. At our very feet poor, fur-
tive Nancy slunk and on this very seat, crouched
panting on her way to her doom. And here
rested Little Dorrit and Maggie, the night they
were shut out of Marshalsea. No, no one who
loves Dickens and thinks he has localized the
scenes the master has so vividly sketched, can
stand here without feeling associated with him,
in spirit at least.

This bridge of solid granite, multiple-
arch design was just a thousand feet long,
twenty-eight between curbs, with six-foot pave-
ments and five-foot parapets, in which on either
side at intervals of a hundred and fifty feet
were sunk recesses four feet deep with granite
seates into which some weary of the incessantly
passing throng might turn for rest.   The bridge
was thus fifty-six feet wide overall.   A tall man
could scarcely see over the regular parapet and
so the recess seats were used for river views,
and as statistics had it, for the strategic opportunity for sixteen thousand lives, and weary of
them, to make a quick dive out of them.

In fact, so popular had this form of exit
from the world become, and so annoying was it
to the traffic under the bridge (for the down-
coming were as likely to hit the traffic as the
water), and, so harrowing to the fine sensibili-
ties of those above it (who were obliged to bear
the ills they had and could not fly to those they
knew not of) that the authorities were planning
to line the parapets with wire netting and thereafter to fine for the first offense, and to im-
prison for the second, any person found entangled
therein.

The main approach to the bridge from
the south, or Surrey, side was the Borough Road
or High Street and from the north, or Middlesex, side, King William Street.   It was, at that
time, the lowermost bridge on the Thames and
over it streamed, at a walking pace, a quarter
of all the vehicular and pedestrian traffic of the
city.   It required strenuous laws to govern the
congestion and during peak hours these were

always insufficient. Its arches were sufficiently
high to permit all kinds of river craft to stream
under, but ocean-going vessels with masts and
the large-funnelled steam craft which were then
coming into use were halted below it. About a
mile below the bridge a tunnel under the river
had been cut to relieve the pedestrian traffic.

Above London Bridge, at varying intervals
of a half mile or so, were other bridges: Southwark, Blackfriars, Waterloo, Westminster, Lam-
beth, Vauxhall, Victoria, and Battersea, and between these were other bridges exclusively for
railway use. The famous Thames Embankment
Act for the improvement of the commerce and
sanitation of the river was already in effect but
only a small portion of the improvement it intended was completed, and that only in the
neighborhood of the Parliament House and Westminster Abbey.

Tide water affected the river as far up
as London Bridge and pushed brackish waters
up much farther, leaving the flotsam and jetsam
of its tremendous traffic on the shallow margins
at each recession. These leavings, together
with flood water, the street washings, and much
of the city's sewerage which emptied into the
river, occasioned a condition best sensed by the
olfactory nerves.

The width of the river bed at our London
Bridge point ranged from five hundred to eight
hundred feet, conditioned by the variation of the
tide. (The purpose of the Embankment Act was
to reduce and make uniform this width, increase
the river's depth, straighten its course, and

beautify its approach; but more than this, to improve the sanitary conditions of the city.   But
this Mother and I did not think of.)

     What we beheld first was the shocking
filthy state of the margins and mud banks as far
as the eye could reach.   To the right was the
warehouse district of Tooley street, which I have
described with the Magdalen school; these warehouses flanked the river and often sank below
its level, each with its wooden, rotting runway
to low water over the viscous ooze, moored to
which were vessels of every description, from
punts, scows, barges, and lighters, up to sloops,
schooners, brigs, brigantines, and full-riggers,
with one six-masted; and then, the black greasy
side-wheel steamers.   Moored to these ships
were others, and to these, still others, until
the shores were forested with masts and funnels.

     Into and out of these vessels that made
England mistress of the seven seas, and up and
down these runways and into and out of these
warehouses, impelled only by the sinew of man,
from daylight to dark and perhaps all night,
every day of the year, poured forth the products
of every clime and land but especially from all
of the lands of the empire; tallow, wool, hides,
skins, furs, pelts, hair, bristles, bone, ivory,
bark, shell, tar and pitch; poured forth gums of
resin, of turpentine, of cowrie, lac, bitumen,
chicle, tragacanth; edible oils, fuel oils, lubri-
cating oils, and medicinal oils; back and forth
men labored under timber: hard, from oak to
ebony, soft, from cork to spruce, and precious
woods, from cedar to sandalwood; forth came
fibers of wood, reed, grass, mohair, cotton,

silk, flax, hemp, and sisal; and raw fertilizers
of animal and fish offal, phosphates, nitrates,
and sulphates.   All of these raw materials, destined for every industry in the kingdom and fur-
nishing a large part of its exports and the major
part of its odors, centered at this part of the
port of London.   It was the nation's ship-chandlery
and the naval storehouse of the world, having
the greasiest, the slipperiest, the smelliest, the
most combustable and most explosive and the
most difficult to transport or handle.

   It was to this very viewpoint where
Mother and I stood, to this very seat, that
Daddy had carried me pig-a-back years before
to witness the "The Second Big Fire of London,"
when this same shipping and these same warehouses were all afire at once and when these
same inflammables were melted and ran afire
right across and down the river, setting afire
the vessels anchored far below.   It had burned
for weeks and the river fire-boats couldn't get
near it for the blazing river.   The melted tallow
and resin and gums had run down the street gut-
ters and into the sewers where it hardened and
clogged them, and this condition had started a
plague from which thousands of people, mostly
children, died.   I remembered how the navvies,
thousands of them, dug in those sewers for
months and drove steam through them for years
to get all that stuff out again.   And, if there
were anything needed to rivet the remembrance
of that scene, it was the picturing of the hero-
isms of the Prince of Wales, a regular member
of the hook and ladder company of the London
Fire Department at the time, who fought as
valiantly in uniform and helmet as any of them

and had some narrow escapes. That, and how
the Department had a great Saint Bernard named
Robin that had climbed ladders and rescued
children through fire and smoke and brought
them down ladders as safely as the firemen; and
how this wonderful dog was smashed by a falling
wall at this fire while dragging an injured fireman out of danger. With great ceremony Robin
had been laid in state and widely mourned, and
given as big a funeral as any hero, the Prince
attending in his fireman's uniform, helmet and
all, and a monument for Robin stands to this day.
These were all fresh memories as we stood on
that granite seat looking toward Greenwich and
they come back to me now at my command almost as fresh.

Looking down the river on the left, we
saw upper and lower Thames Street and Duke
Street Hill dropping from the bridge to the river
level, and similar warehouses and wharves as
on the Surrey side, except that they were mostly
devoted to tobacco products and food stuffs of
more fragrance. Then came Billingsgate Fish
Market, which I suppose has had more stories
written about it than any other market place in
the world.

Looking over Billingsgate from where we
sat, the London monument stood out in gigantic
relief and near it, at a "V" corner near its
foot, was a large cork factory making, princi-
pally, bottle stoppers and life preservers, but
many other things too, including works of art.
It was conspicuous because of a good-sized museum, where were exhibited free pictures, portraits, and miniature buildings, all carved in

cork artistically. Now, it happened two weeks
later that I was employed there counting and
sacking corks at four shillings a week. A month
later found me in a snuff factory next door to it
and in a cellar, putting labels on Old Scotch
Snuff. The label then used has never changed
for I have found it all around the world to this
day.

A few months later I was telling my patron about the conditions in Billingsgate which
so interested him that he said he would visit it
some early morning if I would be his guide; I
could take him to this cork museum at the same
time.

Billingsgate, London's wholesale fish
market, occupied about six hundred feet of the
river front and flanked the beginning of Ratcliffe
Highway on the inside, though the street had
some other name at this point. I became so
well acquainted with this vile place a few months
afterwards that memories rush in to me now of
its hardships and miseries which I would fain
forego but for Mr. Dickens.

The river here has a rude embankment,
paved with cobble and flagging, very rough and
uneven for the purpose to which it was put.
Even my childish mind found fault with it at the
time. It was about two hundred feet wide and
was used as the receiving ground for the hundreds of vessels that arrived during the evening
and night and whose fish must by law be un-
loaded and sold off by 5 a.m., or the surplus
returned to the ships by that time to be destroyed later. Everything perishable had to be

on display in the market building by 6 a. m. and
must be completely disposed of by 11 a. m. The
only furnishings in the building were iron topped
tables on iron legs imbedded in the brick floor,
which was crisscrossed with open drains all leading to the river. Spring-balance scales hung
from iron standards at the end of each table
concession. All conveyances had to be cleared
away by 11 a. m., for at that hour to the minute the fire apparatus with great force of water
sluiced every possible thing entirely out of the
building.

          This made the last few selling minutes
a hectic time for bargaining, haggling, cajoling
and scrambling, for everything, fish, offal,
(and people) were to be ruthlessly washed away.
And of all the filthy, indecent, blasphemous
epithets of all the languages and from all the
throats of every nationality--and from more
women than men, and women the worse--no spot
can vie with Billingsgate. At those minutes just
before eleven this scene was so spectacular that
tourists timed their visits to revel in its excitement.

          Immediately after the sluicing, the out-
side concessions all around the market building
opened up for the sale of such things as shell-
fish and the dried varieties of fish but no more
fresh fish would be seen for the day and the
interior of the market was as quiet as a mouse.

          Long before this hour the little, puffing,
noisy tugs, like so many rooting hogs had worried helpless river craft out into the stream.
Those with sails had set their course down the

river with the wind if there were any, or with
the tide if it were ebbing, or were pulled down
by tugs if there were neither wind nor favorable
tide, or taken in tow, for a consideration, by
foreign steamers outward bound. Those without
sails had necessarily to be towed at least below
Sheerness, for from there on out of the mouth
of the river they must hurry to pass and make
room for their duplicates coming up-river for
the next night's performance. The steam craft
were side-paddle-wheelers, awkward and slow,
and constant menaces to other craft by which
the steamers were hated and harassed.   Ocean-
going vessels of deep draught and passenger type
did not negotiate the river to London, but had
their terminals at the deep-water ports, Southhampton or Portsmouth, and, for the continent,
at Dover, Folkstone, and other channel points.

Looking beyond Billingsgate from our
viewpoint was seen the massive and picturesque
Tower of London with its look of a medieval
castle, and below this on both sides of the river
began the great dock systems, St. Catherine,
Great London, East India, Limehouse, Black-
pool, and many other municipal docks and on
the south side the very large system of the
Commercial and Corporation Docks.   Into the
basins of these systems float the full-rigged
merchantmen, East India Liners, and Atlantic
craft which proudly ploughed the big oceans and
were the pride and glory of all Englishmen.

We could see no farther than this point
as the river began there a big "S" in the curves
of which were the great Woolwich Naval Docks
and Arsenals and the government Navy Yards in

which, and on the river near-by, could always
be found a large part of the British Navy.

From our height on London Bridge, the
moving craft in midstream below seemed darting
and weaving among each other like animated jack-
straws.   There were oarsmen in skiffs, scullers
in punts, coxswained crews of two to six on
whaleboats pulling to merchantmen or from them,
crews in racing shells, solo racers, watermen
in wherries as ferrymen see-sawing from shore
to shore, and swift little penny steamboats that
zig-zagged to and from regular stations on either
side.   There were innumerable little tugs, pushing, pulling, and punting the steam-less and
sail-less like so many bull terriors, all accompanied by the shrieking signals of the penny
boats and the baying of the larger vessels.
Down the center of the river as far as the eye
could see were ocean craft at anchor which
could not find depth sufficient at the wharves.

I think there was no busier port than the
Thames between London Bridge and Gravesend.
I have navigated it in all sorts of craft, swam
in it--filthy as it was, made my living on it,
and twice before I was fourteen was shipwrecked
on it.

Off to the right and a little back from
the river was the huge dome of St. Paul's Cathedral, periodically polished until it glistened
but at most times dismal with soot.   Within,
the cathedral is so majestically solemn and
mysterious that one leaves it with a hushed and
awed memory that lasts throughout life.   Then
to the left we saw the massive Parliament House

rising sheer and gaunt from the water. Beyond
this were the clear-cut outlines of Westminster
Abbey, now chiefly regarded as the sacred shrine
of our beloved immortals, with one of the faces
of Big Ben in the tower warning us of passing
time and its solemn tolling of the hours remind-
ing us our days are numbered.

Here lies now the mortal remains of the
beloved subject of this narrative, my benefactor
and friend. I like to think that the combined
souls of the millions to whom his soul, by his
art and the Mercy of God, brought cheer, com-
fort, and peace, hover o'er his resting place
and I am firmly convinced that the souls of
million yet unborn will live to bless his memory.

Above the din and rattle of shod hoofs
and iron tires on the stone blocks of the bridge
and above the shrieking of the penny boats below, Big Ben sonorously tolled eleven o'clock
and Mother gave me another series of cautions
and admonitions, and then returned home while
I proceeded to Fleet Street.

CHAPTER XVII

The name of the coffee shop to which I
was going I cannot now remember, though it had
reference to the printers trade. To make sure
of being on time I was much too early, so I
used the time in rehearsing my behavior and
speculating on the reason for the summons and
what would come of it.

When my host arrived he was on the arm
of another gentleman and in the company of a
third, both strangers to me. As they neared
me the others were about to say "good-bye"
when Mr. Dickens, catching sight of me, said,
with a wave of his hand, "Ah, Billy! I knew
you'd be on time"; which indicated faith in me.

To one of the others who asked, "Your
little son, Mr. Dickens?" he replied, "No, but
he's one of my boys."

I am careful in recording this incident;
while I am likely to err as to the exact wording
of this, I am sure as to the implication it gave
his departing friends: that he had boys who were
other than sons and who might be proteges or
wards or chums or what-not.

As we passed into the shop, my hand in

128

his, to what I assumed was an accustomed table since the waiter there either spoke to him by name or did some other act that indicated familiarity, Mr. Dickens said to me, "The gentleman who spoke of you, Willie, is Mr. Wilkie Collins."

When we were seated, with the waiter obsequiously hovering over us, Mr. Dickens asked me my choice of the menu but noticing my embarrassment in deciding, he ordered "London grills for both of us," indicating by holding the palms of his hands a certain distance apart something regarding the specifications. I had no notion what "London grill" meant except that it was something to eat, but when it came forty minutes later as a mutton chop the thickness of my wrist and as the waiter said, "Direct from the highly-bred 'o the Downs, sir," stuffed with delicious kidney, crisscrossed with rashers of bacon, and garnished with Cross & Blackwell's pickled walnuts and sprigs of parsley, it put the topper on my steadily increasing appetite.

The "grills" were spread on enormous platters together with the half of a great baked potato of itself a meal; but so long had we waited in contemplation of it and so hungry had we been to begin with, my host as much as I, that right away we buckled into it with hearty good-will and complete success. Ah, the memory of that meat, with its savors and zest has ever abided with me; but, alas: I know I strain the reader's credulity in recording details such as the above so exactly, but I have very tenacious impressions of the hundreds of things that happened in my periods of contact with

Mr. Dickens--to me, great links in my progress.

The purpose of this summons to the coffee shop may have been to simply give me an
unusual dinner, but I am more inclined to think
it was to quiz me, for as soon as the waiter
had gone with the order, Mr. Dickens squared
himself to me with a command. "Now tell me
all about that barber shop where you are working." (This was my first meeting with him
after my mother had told him I was at such an
occupation.)

So I told him, substantially as I have related it here, but as he plied me with questions
that went into minute details he got the story,
with all its vileness, with closer particulars.
To some questions I hesitated, dreading to reveal even to him the revolting conditions, especially as to the sleeping arrangement and the
nature of the food and to the language I was
obliged to listen to, but he pumped me dry on
the subject and ended with: "Your father must
get you out of that," in such a vehement way that
the horridness of it all became more apparent
to me than before. I agreed with him as to
the necessity of a change, especially as I then
showed him the palms of my hands from which
the outer skin was now rubbed off; to this re-
velation he said something which sounded very
much like "damn!"

We then went into the subject of the rehearsals that were now going on at Exeter Hall
and as to how I came to be enrolled in the choir.
This was a much jollier subject which I could
enter with great glee and as I told him under

his intimate questioning of the incidents that led
up to it his exasperated mood changed into a
pleasant one for he laughed frequently.   I told
him how I chanced to become monitor at Magdalen and this led to the reasons for my being at
that school and many particulars regarding it and
its curriculum and its management, and how it
had fallen to me to select the quota, and my inclusion in it, and how at our last annual examination I had inflicted on schoolmates and master
a recitation of a book of a hundred and forty-
five verses entitled "A Mother's Last Words,"
and had received as a prize for this memorizing
feat a large family Bible with a space in its center for Births, Deaths, & Marriages. (That Bible
came to America two years later and was with
all other records and correspondence burned up
in an Indian war in Wyoming.) This recitation
he pronounced wonderful and it amused him very
much.   To test me he bade me begin it and
without regard for time and place--for I seemed
oblivious of anything but my patron--I put myself
in the attitude of declamation and began:

        "The yellow fog lay thick and dim o'er
London City far and wide"; and would I suppose
have completed all of the book had he not laughingly stopped me.

        "Here, Here, that will do; I see you
can do it!"

        There were other things that happened at
that feast that do not connect with Mr. Dickens.
But I recall that both while he was coming in
and while he was going out, several gentlemen
apparently of his literary class bowed to him or

spoke to him as "Charles" or "Dickens." He
seemed well known there. One gentleman had
interrupted our eating for a few minutes in a
business conversation. All of which leads to
an assumption that the coffee shop was adjacent
to Mr. Dickens' business office. I was impu-
dently curious to know what all this luxury cost
but did not see the paying for it, other than to
notice the brazen furtiveness of the honorarium.
A boy always sees that.

On reaching the outside, my host asked
me by what way I had come and I told him and
that my mother had come part way with me and
that we had spent an hour talking about him and
his books.

And then he asked me if I had ever been
to the cathedral and I told him, no, I had
never been on the inside of it. So as St.
Paul's was only five minutes distant he took me
by the hand to explore it.

I remember very few people present that
day but this probably only seemed so because
of the immensity of the cathedral. The vast
distances and heights and the somber tones and
silences gave it an awesome solemnity. Mr.
Dickens was quite familiar with its traditions
and interpreted to me the uses of its every feature and especially of the "whispering gallery,"
and at last we arrived under the vast dome,
looking up to which seemed like gazing into the
celestial kingdom itself. And we gazed and
gazed--at least I did. Everyone knows how it
strains the back of the neck to maintain such a
position; to relieve this, I at last turned my

attention to the beautiful mosaic floor, in the
center of which where we stood was a large,
clear, circular space and the thought irreverently entered my head of what a beautiful place
this would be to spin a peg-top.

Now, and how do you account for this?
Mr. Dickens said, and very much surprised me,
"Have you got your top with you, Willie?"

With the feeling that I had been caught
in a dreadful thought and, more than that, remembering that the top subject was an embarrassing one, I answered, looking away from him,
less frankly than usual.

"No, sir," and then a quick, sly return
to his face found his eyes sternly focussed on
me as though searching my thoughts.

Then this visage quickly changed and he
genuinely shocked me by saying, pointing to the
circle on the floor before us, "Wouldn't that be
a jolly place to spin it?"

"Oh, no! No, sir! Not here, sir!" I
exclaimed hastily.

Mr. Dickens reached for my hand and
we passed on and the top subject passed on and
the incident might have passed on and out of my
mind forever, but for its denouement. Instead,
I never hear of St. Paul's, or a dome, or a
peg-top, without every item of it flooding my
memory.

We left the cathedral, or I did, in a

dazed and sober mood and yet I was inwardly
intensely elated with the adventure. I hope I
properly thanked my friend for the treat and
the instruction as we waited for the bus which
he insisted I must take and to the top of which
I climbed as I waved "good-bye."

CHAPTER XVIII

The way home was again by way of London Bridge, over which it was destined, and in consequence of this visit, too, that I should have some severe experiences, past the London Terminus, past Guy's Hospital, where I was to have some painful remembrances, past St. Thomas' Hospital and on to Bermondsey Street where I left the bus. There was still about a quarter mile to go on that street when I passed a greengrocer's in which also there was a fresh fish market (rather unusual in those days when each shop was a specialty in one line). Attached to the display on the pavement was a sign, crudely painted:

ERRAND BOY WANTED

Now, so thoroughly obsessed was I with the command, "your father must get you out of that!" that the sign seemed to open the gate, and without hesitation I planted myself before a tall stoop-shouldered, seamy-faced man whom I knew to be the proprietor.

"I want to be your errand boy, sir. Me mother buys here, sir. We live in Bell Court, sir" and with intense earnest I pointed in the direction of that locality.

135

The grocer looked down at me, and it
was a long way down, "Oh, you're too little."

Then pausing, and making spectacles of
his thumbs and forefingers, which he held to his
eyes, he said quizzically, "I want a boy twice
as tall as you be."

"Then you want a kid eight two and a
half, sir.   You won't find 'em," was my quick
retort.

To this sharp reply he looked puzzled as
if making a computation for himself.   "Why,
how's that?"

"Because I'm four one and a quarter,
sir; that's half as much."

"Well you're smart at arithmetic anyway," said he; "but really you're not strong
enough," he added, trying a fresh line of objection.

"Yes, I am," I contradicted.   "You
don't know how strong I am, see--" and, just
as quick as doing a sum I gave a lift of something that appeared to be and was quite heavy.

I was very strong for my size and weight,
especially were my wrists strong; my cartwheeling had certainly developed me there.   But, my
poor stubbly-beard-rubbing hands, that Mother
had cried over, that Mr. Dickens had sworn
over; how I did try to hide their palms.

Then, Mr. Henderson, for that was the

groceryman's name, partly won over but not
caring to take the responsibility alone, called
back into the store. "Oh, Mother, come here."

His wife, a jolly looking Dutch woman
who was apparently in equal authority, came out
and was told to "look 'im over, Mother."

Seeing objection coming from this more
critical inspector I pleaded. "You know us,
mum, me mother comes here, she is the loidy
that told ya how to tell cocks from 'ens when
they wuz little chicks, don't ya remember mum?"

This earnest plea brought remembrance
of a comical argument between a fat Dutch
woman and a Kentish dairy lass that excited
much good humor and at last a favorable decision. But there still remained grave doubts of
my strength to pull the heavy truck and to keep
from being "runned over" and to be able to hold
my own with the bullies at the markets, and so
forth, but at length I was told to ask my mother
"to look in about it."

My day's affairs with Mr. Dickens and
the grocer were duly related to all hands at
home. It was decided to serve quit notice on
the barber shop and become donkey to the grocer's cart, a step up in social conditions.

But, the grocer was right. My size was
a handicap and my strength for the job was over-
estimated. The job did need eight two and a half,
brawny strength, and a bullet head to correspond.
I started at 4 a.m. pulling a heavy cart, in the

shafts of which I had to harness myself like a
donkey, over the bridge to Billingsgate by 6 a. m.,
a distance of two miles and partly up hill; there
I would find the grocer waiting and there I would
help him load a half ton of fish.   Then I dragged
through that frightful traffic by 9 a. m. harnessed
to the shaft with breast against the haft of it,
pulling, with Mr. Henderson behind, pushing.   It
was truly a load for a stout donkey especially
up to the crown of the bridge.   This was the
procedure on Mondays and Thursdays.

On Tuesdays and Fridays there were
similar trips to the Borough market for vege-
tables, and on Wednesdays and Saturdays, to the
Covent Garden market for fruits.   It was slav-
ish, arduous work and how cheerfully I performed it is a wonder.   I weighed not over ninety
pounds but because of my tumbling experience
I was wiry and tough and because of stern ne-
cessity--and I think more importantly because
of that dangling hope ever before me that all
effort led to emigration and Utah--I whistled
and sang over it.

I was in a different spirit certainly, to
that which Mr. Dickens described as his own
at my age.   He writes "that I suffered exqui-
sitely in spirit no one ever knew but I" and
"how much I suffered it is, as I have already
said, utterly beyond my power to tell, no man's
imagination can overstep the reality."   And
there are many other pathetic references to the
fact that he was utterly broken and apathetic of
the future.   He refers to his condition as "a
hopeless unmitigated misery."

In respect to this mental attitude toward
life and his condition and environment, my situation offers no comparison. His inherited
aspirations were not mine. His abhorrence of
his occupations and associations were not mine
at his age. His vanity in believing himself in
mental capacity superior to his companions was
not mine. I knew nothing of that dissatisfac-
tion with social conditions, which held his spirit
in "miserable bondage."

On the contrary, I, at that age, with
surely greater reason than he for despondency
(judging by his own measure), never had a fear
of the future, never a premonition of disaster.
As things were with me, they were right. He
had been shy and reticent. This was his demeanor even as a man, as I knew him. I was
fearless, frank, and bold. He shrank from
critical gaze; I courted it shamelessly. He felt
dependent, alone. I think I did not expect even
from my mother anything, not even food, that I
had not earned or tried desperately to earn. I
did not expect from others any special assistance, but instead fought for what I wanted and
usually got it. Mother tells a story of throwing
me into Faversham creek at age two to see if I
would swim, (standing by, herself, of course)
and I did swim, kept my head above water as
any animal will.

And I think this dissimilarity in spirit
and character between us at like ages, when Mr.
Dickens came to know it, is what caused his
chief interest in me.

The job at the grocery taught me many

things that afterward proved useful, such as
putting up packages in cones for everything like
sugar, rice, coffee, and tea, which were sold
in bulk; too, it was my first experience in sales-
manship.   Ten years after this in the other half
of the globe I was one of three brothers in the
wholesale grocery business.

The weekly pay at the grocer's was six
shillings which was an improvement on anything
I had so far been paid, besides many a chance
to get cheap food home.   Also it enabled me to
get home by 5 p. m. and all day on Sundays.
But better than this it gave me time for study
and reading, especially Dickens, which because
of our close association with him now engaged
all members of the family.

This help to the family exchequer was
added to father's twenty shillings as engineer at
the bark mill, Alfred's average, with bonus, of
twelve shillings at the haberdashery, Fred's ten
shillings (with a post peg-top raise) as engineer
in a kid tannery, and Esther's six shillings as
apprentice at a millinery.   This made a family
total of fifty-four shillings (or the princely sum
of fourteen dollars) a week.   As there were
three children younger than I, making seven in
all, and, after tithing, a quarter of all these earnings were religiously put aside for America, it
is one of God's mysteries how the nine of us
lived clean and decent.   It excited the wonder
of Mr. Dickens, too, and he afterwards went
into particulars about it with me.

One morning I failed to report with the

cart either at Billingsgate or the grocery.   A
trace was started for me at home.   Then there
was a hue and cry and a search of the cart yard
which was a mile away in the opposite direction
and there I was found unconscious under the
overturned cart with a load of boxes piled upon
me.   It was slippery weather and I had tried to
pull down the heavy shafts of the cart; had
missed my hold and had fallen on the back of
my head--and the load did the rest.   The accident was directly traceable to my four one and
a quarter and wouldn't have happened to an eight
two and a half and so the grocer and his wife
were morally vindicated because of their freely
expressed misgivings in the first place.   They
generously paid two weeks' wages in place of the
required two weeks' notice to terminate the employment, so, as there was no charge at the
hospital, the accident cost no one anything, but
me a job.

There were no labor laws that regulated
an employee's stature, age, weight, strength, or
occupation.   And there were not many people interested in seeing that there should be while
there were a great many who were interested
that there shouldn't.   Mr. Dickens, who was in
this small minority who were interested in regu-
lating adolescent employment, was very busy just
then in "All the Year 'Round" and especially in
his public readings.   He nevertheless was rais-
ing a stentorian voice and wielding a wicked pen,
enough to disturb the equanimity of the great
majority, on this very subject.   But meantime,
a heavier ass than I succeeded to my job at the
grocery.

And Guy's Public Hospital received me
(now for the second time) and gratuitously and
skillfully mended my fractured skull, my broken
arm, and my bruised body. I give thanks to
family prayers and thanks too for the pot of
tamarind jam from India that Mrs. Henderson,
the grocer's wife, personally brought to me at
Guy's Hospital and for the two pots of Dundee
marmalade which she sent me in addition.

I am glad to remember also that Mr.
Harding, the master of Magdalen, had missed
me at two rehearsals and had made inquiries
and then visited me at Guy's while on his carrier rounds.

We had duly written Mr. Dickens that
Father had got me out of that barber shop and
also about the grocery job, and so we then sent
him word of the accident and that I was at Guy's.
But it seems he was away in the country or
across the channel and did not learn of these
events until after I had recovered. Then he
wrote asking me to report to him the following
Saturday at the stage after the rehearsal.

From then on and until after the concert,
I worked a few days or hours a week as my
strength permitted, on advertised calls for so
many boys or so many each of boys and girls
at Cross and Blackwell's, Soho Square; or at
Peek Freen's Biscuits; or at Christie's Hat
Works. To the latter place on many separate
occasions I went on these emergency calls and
by my zealousness picked up a bit of skill here
and a bit of technique there. In time I learned
a good deal about hat making which I later used

to very good advantage in America.   But there
were also many menial, disgusting, and hazardous tasks, more than David Copperfield ever
complained of--aye, many more.

CHAPTER XIX

I went alone this time to the stage at
Exeter and spent about an hour with Mr. Dickens
in intense conversation: inquisitive and stern
questioning on his part and fearless answering
on mine, for there was never any fear or eva-
sion on my part when with him. He had evidently done some sleuthing for himself as to the
barber business (though he did not tell me so)
either to check up my previous description of it
or to learn phases of it that had not come within my ken, for he showed more familiarity with
it now and questioned me thoroughly regarding
it. Then he quizzed me about the grocery job,
the traffic on the bridge, what I had noticed of
the vicious conditions at the markets, and about
the grocery man and his wife (to whom I gave
good characters), how long I worked each day,
what I did in the evenings, and much more.

On my mind at this interview was the
fact that brother Alfred and sister Esther were
to sail for America in two weeks and that Sister
was to be married on the eve of it, as her
sweetheart, who was a tenor soloist, was going
also. I told Mr. Dickens how we were all excitedly preparing for the trip and how our church
authorities' emigration fund was helping in the
cost of it, all of which seemed to interest him

144

very much but as it was a subject in which I was not equipped with such details as he seemed to want, he instructed me to say, with his compliments, that he would call on Father one night of the following week and that he hoped also to meet the young emigrants, getting from me the probable night when all would be at home.

Mother had put the bug in my ear that perhaps Mr. Dickens needed an errand boy or something of that kind for himself and so, when he was questioning me about the odd jobs I was picking up, I popped the question to him.

He seemed to consider it, but only for a bit. "No. Not yet, boy. What you are doing now with the care you are getting at home is the best for you. All this will be useful to you some day."

No doubt his mind ran swiftly back over a chain of circumstances that had made himself what he was. No doubt he realized that his own wisdom had been acquired, not in the easy road, but in the seamy, hard ruts of life. No doubt he saw ahead for me much danger, hardship, temptation, and discouragement yet hoped and believed that I would the more easily bear them and more surely overcome them by reason of the varied experiences I was then passing through.

Mr. Dickens then led me to the stage entrance of the building and was about to say goodbye when he suddenly stooped, raised my arms straight up, then felt my jacket pockets. "I see you didn't bring your beautiful top, eh?"

Usually quick at repartee, I floundered and stammered. "N-, no, sir."

"Why?" he asked, seemingly astonished.

The question was sharp, unexpected, perplexing; why couldn't he forget that top? Tears forced themselves from my eyes in spite of my effort to prevent them, but I felt obliged to turn them to him. "I, I can't say, sir," I gasped.

That was all. He drew me to him, put on my cap, pinched my cheek. "Well, good-bye, Willie."

And I was gone; but there was something of a thought in my mind just then that if my mother had gone through these motions she would have ended them with a kiss.

I now recall that at first, and usually, when he used my name it was "Billy" but when he was playfully or affectionately inclined it was "Willie."

What with the impending sailing of the "Amazon," which had been chartered by the church authorities to carry the first contingent of "Saints" of that year, most of whom were of the British Isles although some were from Denmark and Holland; what with its carrying off the firstborn, the pride and principal prop of our family, and the secondborn, the new bride, the milliner, my mother's chum, and her handsome and gifted new husband, the tenor soloist, who was booked for the tabernacle choir and who had

just finished his debenture as a shoemaker; what
with the excitement and anxiety of packing for
the voyage of six weeks at sea with all of its
dangers and more particularly, of packing for
the long railway journey in immigrant cars to
St. Louis--which we had heard were little better
than cattle cars and which immediately followed
the sea voyage--and then, for the Mississippi
and Missouri rivers' voyage to Nebraska, which
followed the immigrant cars and then packing
for the most severe strain of all which began at
that river terminal; what with the necessity of
following the hard and fast rules of the immigra-
tion authorities to keep all packing within allotted
space for the ship; within the permitted weight
for the railways; within the proper load for the
river boat; within the prescribed handling of the
prairie schooners, that it might instantly be used
as barricades for Indian warfare; how in the
world could any family manage all this that
didn't have an experienced sailor-man for a
father and husband, a haberdashery ticket-writer
for an addresser, a shoemaker for putting in
the leather bottoms of the dunnage bags and
sewing on the leather hand-holes, and a jack-
of-all-trades (me) to spare?

And who but a sailor and a sailor's wife
could have made those dunnage bags, anyway?
Those great, white, sausage-shaped bags as big
around as a fat man and as tall, which closed
up at the top with a cord and at the last moment
was sealed with wax with the pattern on the
watch-fob of the firstborn. This finality, however, could only come at the instant the carter
at the van hollered "hurry, hurry."

The scrupulous nicety of "just so much
and not an ounce more" that was imposed on
us, and our desire to pack every ounce that was
our due caused endless rearrangements and the
pleading for this and the weeping for being forbidden that, and the repacking many, many times
over and unto the last minute, of three large
dunnage bags for the hold, one hand-size dunnage
bag for the berth, one small box for the medi-
cine chest, one reticule--size not specified--and
one bundle of shawls: the total weight of all
which was limited to three hundred pounds free
on shipboard for each adult, two hundred pounds
on railways, and so far as there was any regulation, as much as you cared to drag on the
handcart. But, excess baggage on the latter
was out of the question as every ounce was a
lodestone.

This sort of packing in a few short years
was being done by hundreds of thousands of
people, who had been living in allegiance through
a dozen centuries to monarchial government and
protected, educated and cultivated by it right up
to the period of Dickens, but who were induced
joyously to forsake it all in numbers greater
than that of the spreading ancient Israelites, and
to journey through a distance far greater and
through hardships and privations more harrowing
to a region so little known that even its nation-
ality was questioned, so desolate that it was
mapped only as the "Great American Desert,"
uninhabited except by savages.

There were thousands that went from out
of London's lowest slums; there were thousands
more of London's workers and shop-keepers;

there were some few from London's upper class; there were none at all from the aristocracy. Also, there were many thousands from the manufacturing regions and the peasantry of the shires.

They left in hundreds of thousands from England, from Wales, from Scotland, from Ireland, all bringing with them the best that is left of the old virile blood of the Briton, Saxon, Norman, and Gaelic, which has made the proud monarchy possible through all the centuries.

But London didn't care--England, Great Britain didn't care. The people that comprised this vast migration had been persecuted at their rooftrees because they had dared to believe and were then shoo'd away with a sneering "good riddance to bad rubbish" as they departed from their native lands. The Bulwark of British Liberty didn't care and so this multitude of clean of heart, honest of purpose, temperate, and industrious citizens were lost forever from the economic fiber of their motherland to found in a rival nation a wonderful commonwealth.

(I often wonder if the attraction of that rival nation had been of a different thing from that of religious belief, if it had been in fact of an economic nature and had enticed only the aristocracy, the nobility, and the entrenched ecclesiastic, wealth and breeding, whether the above "don't care's" would not have been instead dreadfully solicitious.)

And there that night our family was in the midst of it, awed and excited by the impending exodus of Brother and Sister with her bride-

groom, scheming and packing for a journey of
three thousand miles and six weeks by sea,
thence a thousand miles by railway, thence five
hundred miles by river steamer, and thence a
thousand miles by mule-train or ox-train or
handcart, we did not yet know which, through
every conceivable danger of the elements, of
accidents, and particularly of marauding Indians.
At this time because of the Civil War in America the military protection of the western plains
was mostly withdrawn and savages were commit-
ting all sorts of depredations, especially the
harassment of immigrant convoys.

And then, after all the hardship and dangers of getting there, our pilgrims would find
on arrival at their destination that there was
nothing to be found there but the crudest com-
modities hand-made, home-grown, hand-woven,
home-spun, and home-dyed, hand-hewn, and
fabricated there. Remembering this, the reader
will not wonder at the intense desire at packing-
up time to tuck in this little piece of dainty
lace, this pretty ribbon, that tiny heirloom.

"And, and, O, Daddy, please, please
let me take my wedding veil; see? See? Daddy,
what little room it takes? It will, it might--
might come in handy, for--for my first baby,
you know." But the pleading for even such as
this, heart-rending as it was and reinforced by
the tear in Mother's eye, Father's too perhaps,
must have been denied in favor of the sterner,
more practical stuff for pioneer life.

Some of the packing had already been
done on the floor above and some on the floor

above that and now that dunnage on the living
room below must be temporarily got out of sight
for the reception of Mr. Dickens who was due
to arrive and Billy was stationed at the entrance
of the court to watch for him.

CHAPTER XX

I think Mr. Dickens approached us that evening much as would an investigator or a reporter bent on an interview, albeit in a friendly attitude. He must have known something regarding the tenets of the religion of our family, for it is clear that he knew in what way to elicit more intimate information regarding it. In the matter of church support for instance, he learned that our combined income, small though it was, paid a net one-tenth: not from piety, not from force or cajolement, but as a business duty; he saw that we did not begrudge this nor regard it as a sacrifice. He saw the effect of this in the love, peace, and tolerance among us and toward himself and to strangers. He saw jolly animation without boisterousness, recreation without undue freedom, and a passion for information. It happened, quite fortunately for his purpose, that he met a son of Brigham Young then on a preaching mission and our guest for the night.

Marshaling all my remembrance of that evening, I recall Mr. Dickens' general demeanor as reticent and somewhat shy and self-effacing except when he became the professional inquisitor and then he would squarely address himself to his task. His eyes were somnolent and dreamy

in repose or when he was simply listening but
they narrowed and became sharp and searching
when bent on getting into one's mind.   His fore-
head puckered, and his brows lowered and drew
closer when he was vexed or impatient, but only
for an instant.   (I never saw him really angry
but did catch him once getting out of that mood.)

Of course it did not take Mr. Dickens
very long after his arrival to get superficially
acquainted with the family and our visitor and
that before he left, wickedly late for us, he knew
us to the bottom of our consciences.   But, I
must tell what he first did because it affected
the spirits of the party that evening and my whole
life afterward.

We had already supped but the inevitable
billy was handy on the hob and he and Mother
indulged in a cup of tea (none other of us ever
drank tea).

Then Mr. Dickens produced a parcel from
his pocket which from its shape or lack of shape,
gave no indication of its contents.   Holding it up,
he began to relate a story.   It had to do, he
said, with a friend who had a refreshing sense
of sporting humor and a queer way of demonstrat-
ing his affection.   The friend, he said, had lost
a jewel which he greatly prized and under circumstances which implicated a number of persons
in the loss.   However, as it seemed impossible
to locate the guilty one, the friend had generously
concluded to hush the matter completely and suffer the loss rather than hurt the feelings of all
who were innocent; to this end he pledged the
few who knew of the affair to secrecy.   Promi-

nently among this "number of persons" was one
who as yet was unaware of the loss and who if
he learned of it would be greatly mortified and
unhappy, both on his own account and because
he was in a way responsible for all the others.
The friend who had lost the jewel grieved sorely
but silently about this and could not be tempted
to break his resolution to maintain secrecy although every temptation was put in his way to
do so.

    "However, despite his good intentions,"
continued Mr. Dickens, "the secret did out."
The jewel was in some way recovered; how, for
the purpose of his story, did not matter.   It
was now in the story teller's posession and he
thought his Willie boy would be glad to be the
errand boy in delivering it to its owner, with
Mr. Dickens' loving respect.

    With the concluding words the parcel got
unwrapped entirely, for he had been slowly taking off cover after cover during his recital, and
revealed a wonderful ivory peg-top.   The very
peg-top too that had been lost in Windsor Park.
The unwrapping revealed too a grinning Mr.
Dickens, a most astonished family, and a most
embarrassed boy, who, divided between the desires to hug and kiss Mr. Dickens and to hug
and kiss his amazed mother, did nothing but
stammer "thank, thank," and then wept.

    The manner of telling the story, as I re-
call, was very much more rhetorical and mysterious and led up to a much more humorous
and pathetic climax, ending in a way that seemed
to forbid any inquiry as to the manner of recov-

ery of the "jewel": this has ever been a matter
of speculation with all of us.

The conversation then turned to matters
too weighty for small boys even though not a
word passed me unnoticed.   Mr. Dickens seemed
intent only on such adroit questioning as to bring
clear-cut explanatory answers.   From Mr. Young
regarding church organization, the immigrant
fund, the tithing fund system, and so on but
nothing regarding creed or dogma; and from
Father regarding his ancestry,   his sea-faring life,
his present occupation, and his street preaching;
and from my mother about her birthplace,
Wyngham Well in Kent, which he seemed to know
very well together with some legends attached
to it and he said he often took friends there as
he thought it the most quaint and least known
village in England.

Although he had himself been to America,
he admitted that he knew less about it than
most travelers as he had been in the hands of
others who had controlled his movements but he
said he was glad to learn so much about the
vast western part of it, especially about that
part called Utah which didn't seem to exist in
his day.

He was quite sympathetic with the young
emigrants and wished he could attend their wedding but saw it would be out of the question.
But, he would try to see them off when they
sailed from St. Catherine Docks.   (He was un-
able to do either, much to our disappointment,
but he did mail a copy of Martin Chuzzlewit to
the groom, nicely autographed, and a five-pound

note to the bride.)

And last, Mr. Dickens was not satisfied
that night until he had climbed those steep stairs
to each of the rooms above to inquire into this
packing; to examine those dunnage bags; to ask
a quantity of questions and to get a lot of information which seemed to interest him.   He
jollied the young people lightly when they told
him of the horrible things they had been told
they would face and encouraged them by saying
with earnest, "I would well like to go with you."
(And it is all within the bounds of easy credence
that he meant it.)

CHAPTER XXI

Between this visit and the departure of
the emigrants, the time arrived for the performance of the Queen's Choir Concert and so it
was discovered that the auditorium of the Crystal
Palace would not accommodate so vast an audience as expected. For in addition to the twenty-
five thousand members of the choir, there had
been named by the Queen's favor several thousand
distinguished patrons and patronesses from all
over the Kingdom, indeed everyone was clamor-
ing to be invited and so it was decided to use
Exeter Hall again.

It was a wonderful event, excelling, in
its immensity and in the enthusiasm it caused
and in the patriotic fervor it invoked, anything
of the kind ever before attempted. The Queen
very graciously commended and thanked "her
boys" publicly for their performance and particularly for the good behavior and decorum they
had shown.

That the performance could not be given
at the Crystal Palace would have been a greater
disappointment to "her boys" were it not that
Mr. Dickens came to their rescue by seeing to
it that they were each given a book (worth a
guinea) of ten tickets to the Palace and the Ex-

position at Sydenham, good for certain stated
days during the season, including transportation.

     I cannot describe the concert; I was but
a small atom in it.   Its vastness overwhelmed
me.   From my view-point in the topmost gallery
I had but one limited orbit and that, with the
stage as its focus.   Because of my accidental
meeting with Mr. Dickens on the staircase that
day and my interview on the stage (to which I
do not suppose any other of the boys were ever
admitted) and because of the events that followed
I cannot help but regard the performance sym-
bolically as the most notable of my life.   I can
add that if the concert produced the same effect
in the hearts and minds of all the other boys as
it did in me it was well worth the Queen's
while, for although I have been for more than
sixty years an American citizen I have never
failed in my admiration of the land of my birth
and its admirable institutions.

     I have belief that this and other efforts
of this nature in which Mr. Dickens was now
constantly engaged were sapping his vitality. I
do not think he realized how near he was to the
end of fiction writing.   He did but little more
of this beyond finishing the works he had in
hand. (Of course, his very last novel, The
Mystery of Edwin Drood, after several years
off and on with it, and at which he was then at
work, was never completed.) He did not know
how soon his entire time and strength would be
forced into national, civic, and diplomatic work
or that the rostrum in his beloved isle as well
as on the Continent and in America would con-
sume his energy.   His health had not yet seri-

ously failed him but his physical strength, if not his mental ability, was weakening. His optimistic view of everything he came in contact with saw only the intense need and his spirit, only the intense desire, for using his skill, his acquired prestige, his present opportunity of awakening his country to the necessity of certain reforms in education, civic, and criminal law procedures, and in the housing problems of the poor, of eleemosynary work, and better regulation of sumptuary laws. Such work, of course, taxed his writing powers to the utmost and in a much more serious and dangerous way forced a harder strain upon him. I think he often regretted his lack of opportunity of getting back among his beloved creations. I delight in remembering that one day off he had for recreation with "his boys" at Windsor. And I have the fancy that had he lived to continue his fiction for a few more years that we might have seen something in it of our association with him.

After the concert I did not see nor hear of Mr. Dickens for a long time. Perhaps he had gone abroad--as he frequently did--or was engaged in a platform tour through the shires where he was always in request, or in Scotland, for he was ever welcome and much loved by the people of Edinburgh. Naturally we were eager to hear from him. His attitude toward me had inspired strong affection for him but it was regarded as too presumptuous for me to write to him or to look him up.

In the meantime I was employed in all sorts of odd jobs. Some were too filthy for my health; some, too strenuous for my size and

strength; some, too hazardous for my safety.
I worked as a printer's devil and did stage
tumbling; I sold newspapers and fusees on the
penny boats; I went river-diving for treasure.
I even reverted to cartwheeling (on the sly) and
once was solicited by an acrobatic troupe from
a seaside resort, but was not permitted to go.
I could have become a liveried page at Canterbury Hall but could not buy the livery. An apprenticeship was offered me in a lithographic
works but the intended plan of emigration blocked
this too. In all of my inquiries for employment
there was no question raised as to my educational
attainments. At some of them, I think, my personal appearance--which was a little neater than
the average run of boys--and my language, which
was always respectful but applied fearlessly, had
their effect. But I was so young and so small
that no one, apparently, expected anything unusual of me. An exception to this was at the
lithographic works where I did not apply for
the honor at all but was sought out for it because of my aptness in writing and lettering.
Education in those days was, of course, as much
a necessity for success as it is now but the few
who had it were so much in the minority that
it was not looked for, or at least was not expected, from a poor slum boy. Then--

CHAPTER XXII

To my family's great pleasure and to my personal joy came a letter from Mr. Dickens, saying in effect if Willie were not otherwise engaged, and his parents would consent, he would like to take him to his home at Gad's Hill for a visit with his family. That, if consent were given, would Willie come to him on the following day at an address stated (in or near the Strand) to make arrangements, etc.

(This much prized letter was preserved and carried to America but it went up in smoke on the trail in Wyoming along with the Bible and the family genealogy.)

If consent were given? My word! Who would suppose for a moment that consent to such an invitation could be withheld? What a commotion there was! To have waited so long for news from him made this sign of his continued interest in me doubly, triply welcome. To tell the truth, I had begun to feel heartbroken about the lack of word from my mentor and my dear mother realized this. As she could not herself read his writing it fell to me to do so and I acutely remember the tears in her eyes-- and the hug she gave me to hide them--as she remarked my exuberance of joy over the news.

161

So, spruced up and light of heart, to the
Strand I went and found Mr. Dickens in a very
busy office. He was very kind, tenderly kind
for a moment, then led me to a quieter place
and explained that he had been very busy and
sometimes away, which accounted for his silence.
When I expressed in some childish way a fear
that I had in some way vexed him he reassured
me.

"No, I want more of your stories my
boy, but have not found the time or place for
seeing you and so I propose that you go to Gad's
Hill with me next Saturday at noon and visit my
family. I will call at the court for you and you
must be all ready for a quick pick-up. Bring a
little underwear and of course," he added slyly,
"that magic top."

With that he led me out, asking how I
came and when I told him I had walked over
Southwark Bridge this time, he said, "Well, we
can afford to ride back," and put a half crown
in my hand and smilingly watched me away.

Fortune was surely flowing my way that
day. My precarious slum occupations were
ending and aspirations began for a more ambitious career, which, strangely, had never before
awakened. At home, I found a distinguished
visitor, a wealthy lady, who had in some manner
become interested in my father's street preaching, and through that had become quite fond of
Mother and very generous in her assistance to
us. She often found excuses for my going to
her home in Brixton to do some trivial work
and then would send me home with a well-laden

basket of provisions which she called "surplus"
but which was really fresh food from the market.   She was very interested in America and
Utah and came, she said, to talk about it.

     This lady from Brixton listened to my
excited story of my visit with Mr. Dickens and
of its import.   As this brought to Mother's
practical mind the necessity of my presenting a
nice appearance, it also disclosed her worry as
to how this could possibly be brought about and
so advice was asked of the superior wisdom of
the lady from Brixton.   She sensed the difficulty
and finally begged that she be allowed to take
care of that job "as a pleasure to herself."

     When Mr. Dickens halted the chaise at
the entrance of Bell Court at noon next Saturday, he beheld a little boy who was costumed
neatly in a walking suit of tweed--knickers,
buckles, and all--a traveling cap to match,
shoes and hose to harmonize, and in fact a boy
better dressed than he had ever before seen
him be.   The boy was super-conscious of this
and a bit abashed.   The final fitting on and
critical examination of the new apparel had been
going on all morning.   Also the coaching as to
his behavior in company had been going on all
morning and this was superintended by the lady
from Brixton who had taken wonderfully good
care of the job.   The boy was rehearsed as to
his deportment among strangers, toward Mrs.
Dickens, toward the other children, and toward
the servants, and especially as to his table
manners.   Then there were instructions regarding the care of his fine clothes which must be
brushed and folded just so.   And he was told

how he was to address people and how he was
to show his respect to them. Well, the boy
was sure he could and he would remember all
the multiplicity of things he must do, or must
not do, and at just the designated times and
places, too, and in such and such circumstances
and under this and that condition.

And Mr. Dickens beheld a little, bright
blue box, spic and span and new, which was
supposed to contain only the few underwear but
which in fact contained the makings of a most
embarrassing sartorial sequel--and of course
the peg-top.

And again Mr. Dickens beheld the boy's
mother, the dairy lass, the lineal descendant
of ancient Brittany with the violet-blue eyes very
brilliant this morning, and fresh rosy cheeks
vying with cherry red lips, who had spruced
herself tidily to deliver Billy to his host and
who curtseyed prettily and in the quaint shep-
herdess idiom of Old Kent " 'opt her Willie 'ud
be a good boy. "

"An' 'ud keep 'is 'an's clean an' 'ouldn't
get in the woi an' 'ud be respec'ful-loike to
your loidy, sir, " and then imploringly, " 'an
ef ye pliase, sir, ef 'e goes to piratin', send
'im 'ome, won't ya? We carn't a-bear it. "

And Mr. Dickens beheld, and at the boy's
simple introduction, spoke to, the lady from
Brixton who slightly bowed and didn't curtsey.

She graciously said, "I am honored in
personally meeting you, Mr. Dickens, for I

greatly admire the work you are doing. This
little boy will no doubt be much benefitted by
your generous kindness." And then sweetly to
the little boy she said, "So, you see, Willie,
you have brought me a great pleasure also."

The little blue box having now been
placed on the foot-board of the lackey box behind, Billy climbed into the seat, and amid
much waving of hands and good-byes, they
started for Gad's Hill.

CHAPTER XXIII

Gad's Hill lay on the old King's Highway between London and Dover and Canterbury which through all the centuries of recorded history has been the most traveled, the most romantic, and the most tragic road of all England. Most of its way as it goes eastward hugs or parallels the undulating heights of the south bank of the Thames.

As I remember it, Mr. Dickens' home was within a quarter mile of the crest of the river cliff on ground that fell gently from that crest and gently, also laterally, both ways from its own site. From its upper windows and from several near-by but slightly elevated points in the vicinity which are reached in a few minutes, there were comprehensive views looking down the river, with its main channel carrying up and down its heavy burden of city and ocean traffic, its wide margins of swamp lands on either side containing the hulks and skeletons of rotting ships and here and there green islands of low elevations, many scarcely above high tide, which were occupied with dairy farms, market gardens, some industries, and occasionally little towns. At this point the valley in which the river flows varies from a mile to three miles wide, separating the counties of

Kent and Essex, and then widens like the mouth
of a voracious crocodile in profile until it
reaches the sweep of the channel forty miles
below.   The mist, occasioned by the rising
vapor from the river with its large area of
sodden lowlands, prevented at most times a
view of the low Essex shore opposite, while the
same veil of fog, together with the jutting pe-
ninsula of Greenwich, obstructed the view up-
river.

There was, however, no doubt at any
time as to the locality of London.   In clear
weather at Gad's Hill view-points there could
be seen the humidity-laden, sulphurous coal
smoke of the city which rolled and tumbled in
dense mountainous waves, hundreds of feet thick,
bursting oceanward, at every strong current of
air from the interior or from up-river, like the
discharge from the throats of a million cannon,
or sometimes racing like the surge of a cataract
in the opposite direction, when driven by a
strong air currents from channel gales.   When
there was no air disturbance from either way
the heavy pall of smoke settled comfortably
down on the vast city and tucked itself in like
a thick warm comforter, rising occasionally to
show one that the black dye in it was anything
but fast.

But Gad's Hill, although it was not much
more than fifteen miles from London Bridge as
the crow flies, with its two hundred or more
feet of gently ascending elevation happily escaped
much of this nuisance and pollution, so that it
is no wonder that Mr. Dickens had longed for
the ownership of it from the time of his honey-

moon, which was spent in the near vicinity, and,
biding his time, had at last bought it under favorable conditions.

But the vapors from the river valley and
the fantastic and oft-times majestic bellowing of
the city smoke as setting-sun rays penetrated
its caverns, with its then illuminated strata and
attenuated fringes, produced just the chiaroscuro
effect which delights the artist eye.   To this
add the undulating crest of the river cliffs which,
beginning at Greenwich, got higher and higher
until it reached and passed Gad's Hill and then
dropped with a graceful swoop to the river level
again to permit the ingress of several small
streams, which, having converged into the Med-
way, here join the river Thames; having done
this the crest swooped up again, this time in a
more jagged procession, picking up as it went
the chalk formation that became steadily thicker
and more dense until it was the formidable sea
wall of the county on its three exposed seaward
sides.   A fantastic sea wall, battlemented and
castellated, invasion-ready.

Stage coach travel from London to Canterbury and thence to channel ports was by the
King's Highway, more commonly called the Dover
Road, beginning with the Old Kent Road in the
City and running through New Cross, Deptford,
Greenwich, Chalk, Gad's Hill, Strood, Rochester and Chatham, besides many old quaint and
historical towns and villages.   It skirted by
ancient cathedrals, colleges, and manors, with
fine views of rolling downs, private forests and
hunting grounds, wayside inns and taverns made
famous in history and legend by Shakespeare and

other old writers and historians, and now by our own Dickens.

Along this road of broad sweeping curves and many memories we sped, my host pointing out the historical places as we passed them and as we neared his home, he told me I must visit this place and that in the course of my ramblings--that he wished me to do so and to make plenty of inquiry and report to him what I saw and my impressions of them.

But there happened at this time one curious thing. I was seated behind him in the chaise and when he wished to call my attention to anything on the way, he would turn half way toward me, and on one of these occasions just before we reached our destination, in an aside voice he said, "Billy, if my own little boy had known we were going on that Windsor trip he would have wanted to go too. But he didn't know, so please don't mention the subject of the picnic at all while you are here. Do you see?"

"Yes, sir," I answered obediently as though it were a command. But I never did see and even after so many years I am still at sea regarding how little, and why, Mr. Dickens' family knew of such a thing as that picnic day.

It was mid-afternoon of a warm, clear, autumn day when we rolled through the gates of Gad's Hill to the vociferous delight of a number of dogs led by a great mastiff that had evidently been let loose for this event, each dog demanding first recognition and showing no partiality

among their master, the coachman, or me.
And we were met joyously but with more decorum by three of the children of my host who
did show a partiality for their father. And on
a little square portico, embowered in beautiful
rambling roses, that guarded the front portal
of the home, we came to a lady whom I took
for granted to be Mrs. Dickens but whom I later
knew as Miss Georgina Hogarth, (Aunt Georgy,
the children called her) to whom I was presented as "one of my city boys"; and to Edward,
the youngest son, a year or two less than myself, and to Dora about 14, and to Henry a few
years older, I was introduced as "Billy." It
does not seem to me that my surname was mentioned at that time.

Now, Mr. Dickens had undoubtedly spoken
about and arranged for my arrival so that it was
no surprise for them and quite likely he had described my appearance and my dress and manners as he had seen me before my blossoming
out in this new toggery. From this description
the mistress had doubtless determined the ac-
comodations to be disposed to me upon my arrival. But whatever had been, there was then
some inspection of me and some conference
among themselves and then, after certain instructions about dinner, I was taken by a maid,
who I learned was named Ruth, who also took
my little blue box, to a neat little room in the
mansard roof which she introduced with sundry
explanations and departed.

Here I proceeded to follow certain instructions about dinner with certain other instructions from among the hundred I had brought

with me from the combined tutelage of my
mother and the lady from Brixton and after a
very self-satisfied examination of what I saw
in the mirror and the summoning of all of my
dignity, I descended.   Not I think without some
trepidation.

        "Little Lord Fauntleroy" was, I think,
not yet created but thanks to my innate preco-
city and to my recent tutelage and barring the
absence of the swagger-stick of that little lord,
I knew him anyway; I arrived among the assembled dinners dandy, insouciant, and graceful.
And thanks again to these several aids I passed
successfully the ordeal of table manners despite
the veiled and, I thought, amused scrutiny of
all eyes over my appearance.   Not much was
said to me beyond the usual amenities, but this
is the custom at English tables as to children,
who may be seen but not heard, although I
learned that in that household's economics the
Saturday dinner was the gala meal of the week
because it was the only one that the host could
be reasonably sure of attending.

        Although there was no surprise shown
and no comment made on my fine appearance,
there were, I have since come to see, three
separate reasons, each of which had to do with
the amenities of the occasion, why there might
have been both astonishment and comment.

        To the lady my appearance was possibly
quite at variance to what she been led to expect
and it brought a reflection upon her prearrangement of my disposition, which if carried out,
she doubtless felt would have been rather dis-

concerting.

It was a surprise to mine host (as it
was hoped to be and probably was intended to
be by the lady from Brixton) since there had
been no opportunity on the journey nor on our
arrival to apprise him of the contents of that
little blue box, nor to inform him of the wonderful good fortune that had befallen me and thus
have prepared him for my amazing appearance.
He had the interests of each element of the
party to consider and he was best able to judge
its effect.   My belief is, judging from what followed, that it afforded him a little worry and
yet with his faculty of seeing humor in everything he perhaps saw some quiet amusement also.

It must have been a surprise to the
children for no doubt they too had been told
what to expect from Daddy's slum boy, as was
evidenced by their askance yet inquisitive reception of me in the yard.   And here was I,
outshining them in personal appearance at their
own family table.   It wasn't fair; it wasn't right.
They had been deceived.   What to do about it?
It wasn't polite to right such things at the table!
But, there would come a time!

However, youth is volatile and children
have short memories.   The evening passed
pleasantly.   The big mastiff and the other dogs
were admitted and as dogs have no feelings of
caste or degree or previous condition of servi-
tude, nor of pomp nor pride knew they anything,
nor of livery and attire, birth and tradition, nor
name and title were they concerned, and as they
sought my company neither askance nor timidly,

they became the leavening medium between the young Dickenses and me. I learned the dogs' names and their breeds and their tricks and was promised a view of the new litter in the morning and perhaps I might have one of the pups. And I learned that besides the cob which I had seen there were two carriage horses down in the meadow and a shetland pony in the stable that belonged to Edward, but that all the others rode it and I might do so too if Ted, the coachman, would let me. I learned that a governess for Edward came daily and that the others went to school, one to a nearby college and the other to the nearby town of Cobham. This was quite a lot to discover the first evening.

Mr. Dickens had not in any way in any previous conversations referred to his home or his family. There had been no special occasion for him to do so and what I was then learning regarding them was news. During my stay I saw only the children I have mentioned and not much of the elder two of these. Of the other Dickens children, I inferred from vague or over-heard conversation they were married off, away at school, or visiting somewhere. My memory of Dora and Henry is that they were well enough satisfied with me when by questioning they could draw forth from me information regarding my slum life and experience. But since this subject was taboo according to the hundred instructions and the lady from Brixton had edified for me, there was very little of that life that I could conveniently remember. But as for Edward, the youngest and the most lovable and also the frailest, we became inseparable chums at all times, except when the governess separated us. In

exchange for a lot of information about country
life which I surely needed that he could supply,
I did remember for him a lot of thrilling stuff
of sea life and river life and city life all new
to him.

And to this dear boy, who prematurely
passed away a few years later after I had emigrated, I owe the best and the happiest part of
my recollections of Gad's Hill.

Being now countryfied I went to bed early
with a sense of satisfaction in the new role I
was playing and with some lofty resolutions. To
bed, but not before I had brushed and turned inside out and carefully folded those precious,
navy blue velvet-satin knickers and that priceless
pale blue, lined velvet doublet and put that
chevalier chapeau and feather in its paper bag.
All of these togs, as it afterwards turned out,
had received both their christening and their
requiem on that one day. To bed, but not until
I had quoted to myself a pretty thought I had
been taught to sleep with.

It might be interesting to follow one curious train out of these remembrances into
America a little ways--concerning these same
navy blue velvet and silk-satin trousers with
their shining German silver knee buckles fashioned so generously by the lady from Brixton
and worn so proudly and ostentatiously by Billy
the Cartwheeler in the summer of 1864: when,
in America twenty-one years later, huge hoop-
skirts, crinolines and long-flounced pantalettes,
long hair ringlets, and cavernous poke-bonnets

were in full and gorgeous bloom as the height
of fashion for women; and when skin-tight
breeches and long swallow-tailed coats, gaiters
with buckles and stiff bell-top hats, dangling
side-whiskers, dangling monocles, and swagger-
sticks were worn by fashionable men; and when
the graceful minuet was stately paced in triple
measure by both lasses and swains, these same
trousers (laid away, perhaps in lavender) were
exhumed in America by the (same) lady from
Brixton to become the wide-flowing, ballon-
shaped sleeves of a high ruching-necked bodice
of a long-trained, high-bustled fashionable gown
which she then wore to a reception given in
honor of the (same) Billy the Cartwheeler.

And, still more, that same blue velvet,
silk-satin doublet with its robin's egg silk lining,
bright German silver buttons, and hand-embroid-
ered collar and cuffs, became the waistcoat of a
costume worn by Billy the Cartwheeler in acting
in America the character of the doughty, swash-
buckling chevalier, knight, highwayman, Sir John
Falstaff, whom Shakespeare placed on King's
Highway and in that Old Leather Bottle Inn near
Gad's Hill where transpired also so much gaiety
of Dickens' jolly Pickwick Club.

Very early Sunday morning, my first
Gad's Hill morning, I was up and dressed in
my new tweeds as instructed and off with my
host and his sons for a brisk walk, which might
have answered as a preliminary survey of my
coming week's work, for from all of them came
commands to go there or there, the directions
being minutely pointed out or explained.   Then

back to breakfast. But before entering the
house, the other two boys having already gone
in, Mr. Dickens gave me his calling card on
which he added a few words, which was to be
my "open sesame" to everywhere in the neighborhood, and then slyly poured into my pocket
a number of pennies and sixpences and a few
shillings.

"These will last you a week, Willie;
you'll know what to do with them." Bless his
heart! How he did know boys! And how he did
trust me.

A good deal was made of breakfast which
was preceded by grace. The plans for the day
and for the week were discussed and then,
family affairs that couldn't concern me except
that I was to be left to my own devising until
tea time. The chaise and the family would all
be away and some of the dogs too but the maid
would give me a lunch if I returned for it but
that it was the master's opinion that I would
wander far afield.

CHAPTER XXIV

This liberty of action took me at once to the stables where Ted was getting the rigs ready. As he spoke the same old Kent dialect that my mother did and came from very near her birthplace and former home we got along very well. He showed me the kennels and the new litter of pups and when he went to his room above the stable to change his blouse and boots for his driving livery he took me with him.

He pointed to an extra cot in the corner. "Tha' toled un ye 'ud coop wi' me an' a vaited on ya larst e'en an' ya doont coom; vat's oop laad?" Cocking his head sideways and scratching it, screwing up his eyes and pursing his lips, he repeated his inquiry, this time more emphatically. "Vat's oop?"

I explained that I had not known of the plans he referred to but that I had been given a pretty room in the attic.

Looking at me whimsically for a while he then dismissed the subject with a grumpy "huh" which seemed to indicate he was not at all satisfied and that he would think it over. But the thought came to me with some amusement of what a sight it would have been the

evening before if I had sallied forth from the
stable loft garbed in my gorgeous raiment to
eat dinner with the maid and the stableman.
(Oh! the lady from Brixton!)

It cropped out from Ted, the coachman
to me that the maid in the kitchen to him (they
having no bar of social distinction) had made a
number of complimentary references to the
"little lord's appearance" in the dining room.

I had heard so much from my hosts of
Cobham Park, and like any slum boy was so
hungry for trees and grass and flowers and open
spaces, that with Ted's direction I made for it
at once. Its big oaks and beeches were plainly
in sight from the house, especially from my
room, and from the highway that ran between
the house and the gently rising land opposite
which extended to the river cliff. To reach the
park by road, one had to go either east or west
a quarter mile or more before turning down
toward it, but on foot from Mr. Dickens' home
it was easier and more pleasantly reached. One
went by a footpath through the Gad's Hill grounds,
first crossing a narrow shady lane and then going over some small meadows each enclosed in
hedges of hawthorn and with small clumps of
oaks here and there for protection for pretty
gamboling colts in one meadow and the fat downy-
fleeced sheep in the next, and the sad-eyed,
ruminating kine beyond, each meadow filled with
golden buttercups and silvery daisies and sweet-
smelling grasses.

Over the meadows of soft spongy turf that
made me wish for bare feet and slum clothes

that I might pirate a bit; through the turnstiles
and over the hedge-stiles I went and came to
another lane on either side of which were orchards bearing ripening fruit, in dawdling
temptation.   At a crescent curve in the road I
arrived at what I supposed to be one of the gates
of the park which I found was closed and barred
from within and which bore a sign:

RHODODENDRON DRIVE
NO THOROUGHFARE

I did not know what "rhododendron" meant
or if it were beast or plant.   I had been told I
must see the rhododendrons as I had been told I
must see the zoological gardens and I think I had
formed some sort of wild animal impression regarding it.   Within these gates, at a distance of
about a hundred feet, stood a small, quaint-
looking, thatched-roof cottage partly surrounded
by a paling fence and partly embraced by wide-
spreading elms drooping gracefully over the
thatching.   By looking through the iron-work
lacing of the gate I could see that the space
within the palings was a mass of blooms.   One
half of this cottage was two-story; the thatch of
the roof of that half widely overhung and from
its under-gloom were scallopped scoops out of
the eaves, to permit light to enter the peeping,
narrow casements glazed with diamond panes.
Rose and honeysuckle vines climbed over the
walls and roofs and trellised the overhanging
boughs of the trees.

Opposite these gates and on one side of
an open-entrance drive that led toward and then
through a heavily wooded park was another sign,

reading **COBHAM ROAD** and under this in smaller
letters **1/2 MILE TO COBHAM** and over this an
extended digit pointed no doubt correctly toward
that village. But someone, wag or vandal, evidently disputing the accuracy of this announcement, had deliberately and premeditatedly, brav-
ing authority, marred that public sign (and thus
committed a Felony) by placing a figure 1 before
the figure 1/2.

Some time later I and Mr. Dickens, who
strode a wicked pace to keep up with, walked the
distance to confirm either the measurement of
constituted authority or the citizen's dispute of
it, and it took a half hour to cover the distance!
So the wag or vandal, Mr. Dickens summed it
up, if detected, apprehended, tried, and convicted by a jury of his peers, and sentenced by
a perfectly unbiased judge, as he ought to be
for perpetrating a felony, might still find himself, if he happened to have the right kind of a
lawyer in court and a good propaganda agent
outside of court, eligible for a reprieve, a re-
trial, a reversal of judgment, and a restoration
to public esteem, even a laudation and a seat in
parliament for publicly correcting a public mis-
statement and for publicly suffering martyrdom
therefrom.

"At the same time," my host remarked
without once slacking his pace, "it is a sin of
another kind for anyone to cover the distance in
a half hour as we had done, whether it be only
a half mile, a mile and a half, or any intermediate distance and our only excuse for doing
so is to be able to qualify as expert witnesses

in the event the wag or vandal is apprehended
and we are subpoenaed to testify. Even then, "
he added, "so far as I am concerned I would
appear only for the defendant. "

For along this disputed distance are so
many points of interest in real history and so
many more in fable and legend that to consider
or relate each of them separately and ever so
briefly as they were ticked off by so able a guide
as Mr. Dickens, should have led one to forget
time and distance completely.

It was not the main road, nor like the
King's Highway nor the Dover Road with their
noisy traffic and dust; where we had entered it
its name "Cobham Road" began, and the road
passed almost centrally through the vast estates
of Lord Darnley to enter the village of Cobham
and there lost its identity. In going this way it
passed or skirted near to Old Cobham College
or what was left of it and what was restored of
it, including a part of its ancient priory which
was five hundred years old when we saw it (and
a striking example it was of "art in doorways"
for modern architects to copy), and it skirted
the old alms-houses of the church with their ivy-
bowered quadrangles, not quite so old as five
hundred years but still ancient; and then it went
by Old Cobham Church with its fortress-like
tower for a steeple and its ancient graveyard of
great interest to visitors and artists. This church
was opposite the area's most noted place, the
Old Leather Bottle Inn, restored in parts between
Shakespeare's time and Dickens', both of whom
have immortalized it.

On that particular morning, Mr. Dickens
regretted that we could not turn in here but as
we were on our before-breakfast hike which usually took an hour and as we had already exceed-
ed that we hurried for home by the main road.
But I was enjoined by the master to spend some
time at the inn and study the many bulletins and
records it contained and the pictures and quota-
tions on its walls some of which he said one
"must take with a grain of salt."

CHAPTER XXV

But to continue from this first Sunday morning. On the other side of the open driveway leading to the forest and opposite the offending direction sign that had led my host and I to walk off our own measurement, stood another and larger one in the shape of a Maltese cross, the horizontal bar being much wider than the staff; on this was inscribed in large letters:

PRIVATE ROAD

and under this in smaller letters:

FREE ADMISSION
MONDAYS WEDNESDAYS AND FRIDAYS
AFTER TWO O'CLOCK
DURING BLOOM OF RHODODENDRONS

and under this in still smaller letters:

Any Person Detected Cutting or Breaking
Holly or Otherwise Causing Damage or
Trespassing in these Woods will be Pun-
ished According to Law

Hesitating what to do next, for there was not a soul in sight, I peered here and there for any chance of entrance (for had I not that "open sesame" card in my pocket?) and I saw a big

bell high in the trees with a chain dangling from
it within reach.

Well a bell is made for ringing and I
rang it. Its clanger startled me in the drowsy
silence of the woods, a desecration of something
sacred, when I saw a little girl coming with a
skip and a hop from the cottage toward me. As
she neared the gates I decided she was a pretty
girl, remarkably pretty, even though she wasn't
all dressed up and even though her hair did hang
in pig-tails. I resolved that she was about my
own age and that her hair would be in long,
golden-brown ringlets if released. As she reached the gate, with a bound she sprang up it a few
feet, hooking her legs and her arms in the bars
of it much as a monkey would, and, being so
perched, proceeded to catechise me.

"Who be you, eh? What d'ye want, eh?
Ya don't belong 'round here, d'ye?"

This volley of questions did not bid for
an immediate single reply. Interrupting these
triple shots I finally got out "I live with Mr.
Dickens, I--"

"Naw ye don't, naw ye don't; I know all
on 'em oop there," indicating with her head and
shoulders the direction of Gad's Hill.

"But," I persisted, "I've just come, I,
I'm one of his city boys--see! Here's an order
to see IT!" pointing to the sign overhead for
the rhododendron IT, and holding Mr. Dickens'
calling card toward her.

This she snatched through the bars for
all the world just as a monkey would and tried,
or pretended to try, to read it.   Failing in this
she somewhat mollified her tone.   "What do ut
soi on it?"   She handed it back to me.

Now the fact was that I had previously
tried to read the card myself and could not make
out the writing on it so that there was no wonder
that she failed to do so.   But, it had to be read
and under the circumstances I felt justified in
giving it a high sounding message.

With a legal twang I read it.   "The bear-
er is entitled to a view of all things and to enter
all gates and nobody must stop him."   I ended
imitating her imperial tone.   "Well, an' who be
you, eh? so high an' mighty, eh?"   Then, influenced I suppose by the peace and content of
all nature around us, I pleaded.   "Please, please
let me see the ro-do-do-drons an' I'll tell you
my name."

Amiability soon prevailed and I told her
my name and shook hands with her through the
bars, from which she then descended and let
me in.   I told her frankly that I didn't know
what a rhododendron was like nor much of anything else of country life but that I was glad to
have such a pretty girl as she to show me.   By
such ingratiating means I learned that she was
the youngest daughter of Thomas Elliot and that
her father was the flower gardener for Lord and
Lady Darnley of Cobham manor; that the cottage
was the park "Lodge" and her father lived in it
rent free, being a servant of the manor, and
that likewise they had their milk and butter and

eggs and honey and lots of other things free,
and that as she was a daughter of the lodge-
keeper, she was the official gate-keeper--this
was always the custom. She knew all the
people of the countryside, including the Dickenses.
She told me that Mr. Dickens came often to the
park, usually before breakfast, sometimes with
strangers or with his boys but oftener alone except that his dogs always came with him and
that she "just loved him" and that he called her
his "Woodland Maid."

          "Why didn't he coom wi' ye 'imself,
'stead 'o sending ye all alone?" she asked in an
aggrieved tone of voice.

          And then she proposed that as keeper of
the gate, which at that time of the day was seldom used, and having no chance that day for
Sunday school, she would take me around a bit.
She took me to such a profusion of rhododendron
as made the park the showplace of the whole
countryside, and to beds of other blooming
flowers and to ferneries and to shrubberies the
names and varieties of which she freely recited
but which, of course, I cannot remember, and
to hot-houses and nurseries; and she took me
into groves of wonderful trees where we seemed
lost to the world, and to ponds where water
cress grew, and to springs of water in the gloom
where she pulled delicate ferns and wove them
in her hair, and then to fruit orchards where the
temptation to dally was not this time ignored.
She told me the history of each tree and variety
of greenery we came to.

          It was well past noon when we got back

to the Lodge, very amiable friends now. She
seemed to know everything about nature; she was
nature's most amiable product, looked it, talked
it, and seemed to feel it, and she gave me more
information about it than I would ever be likely
to acquire of my own seeking. While I, knowing
more of the city than she would ever be likely
to learn found her equally interested in my
stories.

I did not need to return to Gad's Hill for
luncheon for on reaching the Lodge we found the
Elliot family waiting for the gate-keeper's
daughter and the city boy of Dickens' with a
bounteous farm-cooked dinner drawn from all of
the resources of the most extensive and best
preserved manor gardens of Kent.

In the next two weeks I had so many adventures in other parts of that delightful domain
that I was able to enter that intriguing Lodge
but once again despite its many attractions and
invitations.

I arrived back at Gad's Hill dutifully before the folks arrived and was instructed by the
maid that I was to tidy myself and get ready for
dinner but "as there would be no company," and
this was impressively said, I "need not wear my
pretty chevalier clothes again"; an admonishment
I suppose she had been instructed to deliver.

As the reason for my not having appeared
for luncheon, I told her about Mr. Dickens'
Woodland Maid and of my delightful entertainment at the Lodge, to which she laughingly said
she had never been down there yet but she

thought she would like to look into this "maid" business for herself.

Later, at the table I was asked to report my doings of the day and had great difficulty in subduing my enthusiasm over the story, hitting only the high-lights of it but including the Wood-land Maid part, which greatly amused Mr. Dick-ens who then told the family more about her and her father.

"And did you tip the little gate-keeper?" he then asked me.

This astonished me no end and abashed me more, for such a thing had never occurred to me, and if it had, however much I would have wished to do so I would have regarded it as too presumptuous. Some simple answer of this sort I gave to him. But he corrected me.

"Oh, no, that's how gate-keepers make their living; don't forget next time!"

I was silent, feeling guilty of having com-mitted a social blunder. Yet, what should a slum boy dressed in tweeds know about tips to gate-keepers? Not one of the hundred codified instructions appertained to such a situation. And I wondered, had I been dressed in the velvets, would I have known?

CHAPTER XXVI

These younger sons of Dickens as I remember them, who were at home at Gad's Hill,
were keen on sports but with such sports as my
experience had had nothing to do. They knew
all about cricket and conversed glibly about it.
But cricket is played on greens and I had seldom seen greens and more seldom had I ventured upon them so that I could not hold my own
with them about it. This was true also of ten-
nis and of riding and horse racing, as well as
other outdoor pursuits and this somewhat isolated me from their conversations. But on the
question of athletics and prize-fighting and foot-
racing and of marbles, shuttle-cock, and especially peg-tops, I had the advantage. This,
together with the rumors that had sifted in to
them of my professional reputation regarding
cartwheeling, hand-walking, rope-climbing and
so forth, and the specimens of these that I
moderately exhibited, put me somewhat on a par
with them. I had not been requested by my
host or hostess to subdue my pirating 'abits
but they knew of my instructions from home
and they recognized my intentions to obey them.

After breakfast the next morning as suggested by their father, and having an hour before
school, all three of them including Dora took me

over the premises, showing me all that I had
not seen before. We went through a subway or
tunnel that ran under the highway with pretty
climbing roses at either end, and through the
rather extensive grounds beyond to other roses
in beds and on bowers and arbors. Then we
went to the vegetable garden and the berry patch
and the orchard, all of which, it was told me,
were under the care of Ted and a young gardener who helped him. And all the time I was
keeping my eye out for a suitable site for a
peg-top tournament. Spinning tops is a sport
which has its seasons like straw hats and winter
furs, and that season was then coming in.
Finally I found the perfect place on a small
stretch of flagstone pavement at the entrance to
the home on the highway and here we agreed on
a trial of skill that evening.

Edward was too frail a child to be boisterous at anything. I was not warned of this
but the fact that I understood, and that I led
him only into such games and entertainment as
were safe for him, was I think appreciated.
Henry was delighted with the peg-top and of all
our games he enjoyed spinning it most, doing
it so skillfully that in the end he had won my
ivory beauty despite a demurrer from his father
who carried the romance of it in his mind.
However, in the interests of a sporting propo-
sition and fair play, his objections were at
length overcome. And so ends the story of the
peg-top so far as I am concerned, but it always
gave me a pleasant thought that it had passed to
so appreciative an owner.

The next day I was initiated into the

saddle. Although I had ridden an elephant, a
dromedary, and a giraffe at Windsor, and these
and other show animals at other places, some
of it in the course of my pirating, I had never
sat on a horse, a pony, or a donkey. I had
hardly had a chance to stroke or pet them other
than to hold their heads for mounting, or for
visitors at curbs, for sixpences and shillings,
and never had I curried or cleaned one or had
anything to do with stables. But I now had
Edward's consent, provided I could get Ted's,
not only to ride "Ginger," for that was the
Shetland's name, but to care for him while I
would be there, for the experience it would give
me. By this time I could palaver Ted into almost anything. He taught me to handle not only
the pony but the cob as well and such attentions
to the carriage horses as my size and weight
would permit. Indeed, he laid the foundation of
a new trade for me.

There was not much risk with Ginger.
He had received his name, his master told me,
in the hope "that it would spunk him up a bit,"
his natural disposition being as mild as a cu-
cumber's. He had the utter disregard for pleading by voice, spur, or gad that any donkey ever
had and the same inclinations as regards hurrying or moving over (or standing still when one
wished him to). Ginger had come to Edward
with that reputation when Edward was only six
and there had not yet come any temptation strong
enough to induce him to break his ways. He
had also come with his own opinions and he still
owned them. He had come when his present
disposition had suited the necessities of Edward's
age and strength and he did not develop a differ-

ent one to meet his master's growing needs.
He did not evolve; he was a fundamentalist.
His chief virtue was that unlike the worm he
would not turn when trod upon. But, bless him,
he carried me many a mile. And I always
made it a point to have him, at home, clean
and ready for any of the children who might
want him. Five years afterwards, when I was
night-herding and cow-punching on the plains
and in the mountains of Wyoming and Utah, I
would think of Ginger and my initiation into the
saddle with much amusement. And I named my
first bronco "Ginger."

Mr. Dickens remained at home most of
the following week and was busy writing while I
went wandering from shortly after breakfast until
tea time. Always in the evening I was urged by
special suggestions that I should go to this or
that on the morrow. I do not think Mr. Dickens
had special hours for his work, and perhaps he
was hardest at it when he seemed most idle: at
work thinking. His actual writing when he was
at home was done partly in his library, or den,
which led off from the drawing room (and which
I never visited) and partly in a little pergola,
canvas-lined within and vine-covered without,
which stood about fifty feet below the house away
from the highway toward the stables and kennels,
the intervening space being lawn and shrubbery
and flower beds.

I sometimes worked in these beds, under
the charge of Ted and sometimes on other matters at the stables if he asked me to. But I
was wholly free and was expected to make the
best use of that freedom. And so it was only

evenings and early mornings that I saw the
master, except occasionally when he would sally
forth alone for a little while as though to get
exercise, or possibly inspiration. Nothing was
ever said in my hearing that I can recall as to
the nature of his writing, but as Our Mutual
Friend was the next work he brought forth I may
assume that I saw that in the making.

But, on one occasion which could easily
have escaped my memory but for its sequel ten
years later, Mr. Dickens picked me up from
something I was doing on the grass or flowers
and bade me come with him. He led me through
a narrow tunnel that run under the highway and
up on to the land opposite to what he said was
his rosary, where there were some trellised
bowers completely rose-covered, and then through
a hedge and some clumps of wood and open
spaces to a promontory which gave a broad view
of the Thames toward its mouth.

Mr. Dickens was hatless, in a light,
loose house-jacket split in halves up the back
which the wind persisted in blowing backward
so that the two halves resembled the wide-spread
pinions of an eagle. He pointed out objects in
the stream below and he asked me about some
experiences I had had on the lower reaches of
it. In some previous conversation I had mentioned these experiences to him, being shipwrecked, for instance, down below Sheerness.
And then he told me of some of his own cruises
down there when he had been searching among
the hulks and muddy margins for data for his
stories. Then the conversation changed in some
way to feats of memorizing and being out of ear-

shot of anybody he made me recite some things
I had declaimed at school, which included that
old loyal American inspiration, "Old Ironsides,"
and that other British inspiration, "The Departure of Marmion," and then an old Eton Rhyme.

When he had had enough of this to suit
his purpose he said, "Billy, if you were not
going to America I would make an actor of you.
But," he added, "you had better forget "Old
Ironsides" until you get over there."

Ten years after this conversation I was
a part of a wonderful dramatic organization in
America wherein memorizing was an important
factor and for which I enacted the parts of many
of Dickens' characters, notably from Oliver
Twist, A Tale of Two Cities, The Old Curiosity
Shop, and Little Dorrit, and I had assisted in
dramatizing David Copperfield under the title of
"Little Em'ly"; I was able to portray these
characters with more feeling and with more inspiration and understanding, I think, because of
my familiarity with their creator and perhaps
also because of that very day on a promontory
of the Thames.

CHAPTER XXVII

A few days later a foreign-looking gentleman arrived to be a house guest for a few days
but unfortunately just when Mr. Dickens was obliged to be absent.   He was a new acquaintance
of our host and an artist by profession.   His
appearance was scholarly and his manner was
temperamental, but I cannot remember his name
which had a foreign sound.   With an apology to
the artist, I was made a makeshift for a host
and a substitute for a guide, so that he might
visit such sketching points within easy reach as
had been pointed out to me or that I had found
by myself.   With this feeling of importance, I
first piloted him to the promontory where Dickens had taken me for the declamations and that
comprehensive river view and repeated to him
some of what our host had told me about the locality as scenes in some of his stories.   I told
him that we had named the spot "Inspiration
Point."

As the artist settled himself to paint and
as he did not talk while working and as he expected, he said, to remain there until luncheon,
and as I had a definite project of my own under
consideration which had been conceived the evening before, I got excused, and wandered down
the declivity of the river cliff to the marshes

195

below.   It was a brilliant day; such a day as
would dispel fear, banish ghosts and ghastly
visions of fierce-looking pirates hanging in gib-
bets, and do away with escaped convicts hungry
to the point of eating the livers of timid little
boys--but I had just read the opening chapter
of the book my patron was revising, and could
easily fancy how the scene would appear in the
gloaming of a rainy day to a frightened and
threatened child in a murky, moss-covered
churchyard among the graves.   The birds everywhere shrilling for recognition and cooing for
company warmed a shiver.

        I passed over several old bridges, all
awry, that went over several little streams and
then through a marsh over some stepping stones
green with slime, but in the sunlight, oily and
iridescent;   and up a slope and through the winding lane of a little village that hugged the hillside
and might have been deserted it was so quiet,
and passed a tiny, old, squat church with a
thin, steep steeple and by a moss- and vine-
covered wall of big round stones.   Stones so big
a giant must have laid them up and so irregular
that the giant could have had no system but
probably laid them up with the thought that a few
centuries later some sentimental sketch artist
would come along and fancy he could see art in
it, and make a picture of it to illustrate some
gruesome tale in a book called Great Expectations.

        I continued up the course of these
streams to their origin, a little river, and to
a more open and less damp country, and soon
was in the very pretty city of Rochester with
its majestic cathedral and world-renowned old

architecture. I had been told what I must visit
and went to it, but I used part of my time there
also, perhaps a good deal of it, among the
ribbon shops.

Returning this time by way of Cobham,
I explored many places into which my inquisi-
tiveness carried me as well as some that were
made famous in history and story, including an
hour within the Old Leather Bottle Inn. Here
my open sesame card came in good stead and
furnished me with refreshment and rest, of
which I was by then much in need; and later,
it brought me a tour of the yards and stables
with a book of historical information about the
place as well. My guide pointed out the many
bulletins and epigrams and the old postings of
obsolete rules which lodgers and servants had
had to follow and gave ready replies to my
ceaseless questioning until I was happily satu-
rated with Jack Falstaff and his maurading gang;
with Dick Turpin and his merry highwaymen;
with Tom Sayers and Jack Heenan and Jim Mace
each in turn world champion in the noble art
of bare-knuckle prize-fighting. All of them had
been honored patrons of the Inn. The innkeeper
told me about the jolly individuals and groups
with which Mr. Dickens had peopled it: Pickwick and his friends who were just as real to
me as was anyone. To prove it, there were
the autographed signatures of them in the guest
books, and there were the souvenirs of furni-
ture and implements they had used, and hand-
writing they had left, and pictures of them innumerable. I doubt if there is any other fictional
character who has been picturized as much as
Pickwick.

I was a tired boy when I reached Gad's
Hill again, having done about fiften miles,
every inch stuffed with romance. I had, in
addition, executed an important mission which
was also somewhat romantic.

Prior to this, the day before, it must
have been, feeling the need of advice and sympathy, I had confided my social short-coming
regarding the Woodland Maid gate-keeper's tip
to our maid, Ruth, at Gad's Hill. She, perhaps
covertly enjoying my embarrassment, advised
me that a prettily made-up tress ribbon, as they
were then called, would be just the thing to make
amends. They could be bought at the fine shops
in Rochester, she said, and would solve the
problem she was quite sure, if presented in a
nice way (which, she thought, I was capable of
doing). The advice appealed to me but it presented another problem; how an inexperienced
boy like me would be at shopping for tress ribbons. However, when I deserted the artist at
Inspirational Point the next day, it was because
I had gotten the inspiration to do some shopping
for myself at Rochester. And so when I arrived back, tired and dusty, the last half of the
problem had been solved (getting the ribbon) and
the first half (giving the ribbon) was solved in
my dreams.

CHAPTER XXVIII

I had been writing a chronicle of my adventures every night and mailing it to my parents every morning but it was not expected that I would hear from them often. But on this next day, the tress ribbon day, came a letter from Father to say that all was well and which ended, "tell Mr. Elliot that our son in Utah has sent us some bulbs which he says are the tubers of the state flower of Utah, known as "sego lilies." We have no way of growing them here in London and he may have them with our compliments if he cares for them."

As this postscript fitted in with my dreams of the night before and as the artist was expecting me to take him to another site for his sketching, I explained to him in glowing terms, for a child, on the beauty and quaintness of that old gate and Lodge at Cobham Park. My fervid description captured his imagination and so, after I retrieved the tress ribbon from Ruth, with whom I had left it for examination and approval, and who had examined and greatly approved it (and who said in fun, "You ought to wear your prince's dress for that job"), we, the artist and I, started across the meadows and stiles and through the shady lanes for Cobham road and the Lodge gates.

Hitherto I had thought the artist somewhat
phlegmatic and unresponsive to the witcheries of
nature but from the time I described the gate
scene and until we reached it, he had been much
more free with his conversation.   At several
places along the path he had paused, seemingly
for the estimation of groupings and postures of
trees and animals and the backgrounds of light
and shade, talking volubly meanwhile.

Arriving at the gate he fairly raved.
"Boy! You did not tell the half of it!"   He
averred he could see pictures in every direction,
that he would surely be there most of the day,
that I might watch him if I wished to, which I
appreciated as I had not before been invited, and
to bring him a lunch later.   As he was arranging
his set-up, and being obsessed with a sentimental idea connecting Mr. Dickens with the
place, I told him about the Woodland Maid and
that she was the gate-keeper and would have to
let us in as no one else was permitted to open
the gates.

"And, oh, sir, she'd make a pretty picture for you, my word!" With that I clanged the
bell which woke up echoes from the opposite
forest and added the art of melody from the lovely
silence to the art of color in riotous and beautiful blendings, which everyone knows makes a
dangerously romantic combination.   And then two
chubby, ruddy-faced, towsie-haired young un's
came a-running, waddling rather, with wide trousers to their heels and long smocks to their
knees, recognizing me.   This was a little different picture from what I had expected from the
ringing of the bell and it was different from what

I had led the artist to expect and he said a bit
sneeringly as he pointed to the young un's, "So!
This is the Woodland Maid, eh?"

The young un's said "'Ullo."

"Hi! 'Ullo; er, where's Emma, eh?
Where's the gate-keeper, eh?"

"Gone!" said the young un's, laconic;
I heard a tone of finality.

"Gone?" said I, despairing, with a vision
of a tress ribbon in my pocket and of an unre-
quited social obligation. An anticipated pleasure
had come and faded like an evanescent dream.

"Gone?" I repeated, "Gone where?"

"To post," said the young un's and began
scrambling up the gate.

"And where's post?" I entreated, relief
dawning.

"Down there," chubby fingers pointing,
"to Cobham."

The birds overhead sang as sweetly as
they had before the rude bell had hushed them
to silence for its echo.

As I amused the young un's through the
bars of the gate, as we think we amuse caged
monkeys, and watched the artist lay out his
things for a series of sketches ("to tell it all,"
he assured; not simply "a half of it"), I re-

flected that Cobham and the post were after all
not very far away and that my pretty gate-keeper
had most likely gone to mail letters, which
wouldn't take long and that she would be back by
noon, anyway, and just in time perhaps for me
to cajole from her the artist's lunch--never mind
myself; I would be busy with other things less
prosaic than lunches.

It was not through these gates but through
the park drive opposite which would lead to the
flower gardens and work shops of Mr. Elliot,
as well as to Cobham Hall and so, after watching
the artist sketch in the young un's from their
pose half way up the ironwork, roly-poly as
butter-balls and near enough alike to be twins,
and after giving the artist my opinion that I
could forage a lunch for him at about the right
time, I turned into the forest in search of the
gardener and for any likely scene for a sketch
for the artist.   In time I found both.

Mr. Elliot was mightily pleased with
Father's offer of the lily bulbs, telling me he
was gathering wild tubers from all over the
world and that he would look into the history of
these "sego lilies."   (Before I left England he
was growing a much more beautiful blossom with
them but with a less edible tuber than I afterward found in the wild ones of Utah.)   Mr. Elliot
was, like my mother, of Kentish yeomanry and
well-educated also but he had retained much of
the delightful Kentish accent.   He was a specialist
in bulbs, ferns, and crotons, and took me to a
lovely fernery to prove it and kept me busy ex-
ploring among his treasures and giving me a lot
of information until time for luncheon and then

he bade me go home with him for that repast,
just the thing I was wishing for.

On our way to the lodge I introduced the
artist who was then also invited but he excused
himself saying he preferred to stick to his work
as he was fairly in the swing of it and would be
better pleased with just a snack. We entered the
Lodge grounds not through the gates but through
a cleverly concealed gap in the hedge about a
hundred feet distant from the gate and toward
Cobham: it led first into a bit of a maze and
ended with a turnstile, easy enough for a human
but impassable for animals and this was what it
was intended for.

"It is by this entrance," said Mr. Elliot,
"that Mr. Dickens comes to visit us."

At the Lodge we found that the maid had
not returned but surely would in a few minutes.
The snack for the artist, by its appearance of
bulk and weight on a good-sized wooden trencher
was sufficient to surfeit a gourmand, but I later
found that the Elliots were used to doing things
on a large scale. As I placed the trencher on
the folding stool which the artist vacated for the
purpose, I noticed he was far along with his
work, having completed two sketches, and was
working now on the gate itself, intending finishing up with the Lodge in the afternoon. That of
the gate, drawn partly ajar, was on the easel in
outline only. And the outline was blank in one
portion of the gate for I had told him in part of
my meeting with the little gate-keeper and of her
story of being the Woodland Maid of Mr. Dickens,
and the artist wanted to sketch her in it as I had

described the scene.

And just then, down the village road I
espied the object of his (and my) wish approaching the gap in the hedge and I hastened, with my
hand covering the little package in my pocket, to
meet her. At the stile within the maze--and did
you ever happen to notice what a sentimental thing
a hedge-stile is?--the package was unpacked, re-
vealing a neat little made-up bow of autumn ribbons that well became her golden-brown hair,
now flowing free, and harmonized too with the
hues that nature herself was just beginning to
wear. The presentation of the tress ribbon and
its acceptance were mutually satisfactory but it
took some time, in fact it delayed our arrival at
the dinner somewhat.

I told the Elliot family of the artist's desire to include the gate-keeper in the sketch
which, I took the liberty of adding, was no doubt
intended for Mr. Dickens himself and so obtained
their consent. It had already been planned that I
was to return with the father to Cobham Hall to
view it for myself and to meet Lord Darnley if
he were there, or Lady Darnley if she were there,
and to get consent, which was always necessary,
for sketching the mansion and its grounds on the
morrow. But, although I gained the consent in
this respect, the morrow's visit never came about.

When I returned to the road the artist had
packed up and was gone, but seeing him retreat-
ing in the distance I hurried to overtake him and
tell him about my success at the Hall.

Late that evening, Mr. Dickens returned

home and after a lonesome late dinner (we had
all dined already, not expecting him) the artist
showed us his sketches of the day, all in the
rough to be finished later or used as copies for
other paintings.   There were five of them;   one
of the road looking toward Cobham with the
square medieval tower of the church in the distance, one of the old thatched Lodge itself, one
of the gates closed with the young un's perched
upon it, and one of the gates ajar with a pretty
little girl in neat dressed-up attire, with golden-
brown curls with a pretty autumn-tinted tress
ribbon in them, and with a sun hat carelessly
dangling at her side.   Pretty enough composition,
no doubt.

        "This is your Woodland Maid, Mr. Dickens, "
said the artist, at which the master, glancing
from the picture to me, his head bent sideways
in a wise attitude of approval, fumbled his hands
one over the other as though in doubt and said:

        "So, oh?" and "how do you like that,
Billy?"

        I had formed an opinion and was ready
for an answer, but was a little afraid that mine
might not meet the general verdict, so nervously
I said, "It, it's pretty enough, sir, but I'd
rather see 'er in pig-tails and bare feet, a-
gibin' at me through the bars like she did afore!"

        "So-oo!" said he, in the same tone as
before, "So! You've seen her before, eh?" and
then, as though remembering that of course I
had, he added, "By the way, Billy, did you
square yourself with the little gate-keeper about

the tip eh?"

   For answer I simply pointed on the picture
to the tress ribbon which the artist had played up
with conspicuous fidelity. This must have been,
for them, a comprehensive answer and more re-
vealing than a burst of oratory for it brought from
the questioner a slowly repeated nodding of the
head as though the head were too loosely attached
to the spine and brought the lips to a whistling
position as though about to let off steam, the
brows down as though in a quandary, and the eyes
to mere slits as though focussing the mind on a
weighty problem. After all this preparation the
only audible result was a prolonged "o-o-o" from
him. And the artist, who from watching all these
antics, discovered that he had unconsciously
painted in a bit of sentiment as well as a bit of
landscape, contemplated this feat by stroking his
nose with his forefinger and thumb as he nodded
his head in unison with the head of the host, and
emitted a prolonged "a-a-ah." And the children,
constrained from audible opinions, more adeptly
answered with significant glances.

   As an illustration of how intimately are
the threads of life woven in this world and as a
corroboration of my remembrances of that short
visit to Gad's Hill I have recently visited at
Long Beach, California a Mrs. Emma Packman,
a widow lady of seventy six who is yet well and
hearty and who was the Emma Elliot, the "Woodland Maid" of Charles Dickens, the daughter of
Thomas Elliot, the florist for Lady Darnley of
Cobham Manor and the official gate-keeper of the
Lodge of Cobham Park, Cobham, Kent. I had
first met Emma Packman in America as a visitor

to the Dickens Fellowship of Los Angeles.

I have read to her this part of my narrative, which she laughingly admits might all be
true as she distinctly remembers that Dickens
called her his "Woodland Maid" and often visited
the park, usually in the early morning; that he
often had his boys or visitors with him and always
his dogs; that her father was the floral gardener
for Lady Darnley and likely knew Dickens very
well; that it was very likely that he sent choice
specimens of his flowers to Gad's Hill, that artist
friends of Dickens as well as other artists often
came sketching the Lodge and gate and Hall.
That perhaps she was a pretty girl and did wear
her hair in pigtails and in ringlets too.   She
wasn't so sure about the bare feet, as the ground
was too rough with slaty rock thereabout and besides she did not think Lady Darnley would approve of it.   But she did show people around and
got tips for it and possibly hair ribbons as it was
a common practice with gate-keepers' daughters
and the way they earned a little money.   And it
was natural enough that a little friend of Dickens'
who was hungry enough and who happened around
just as the family were sitting down to a Sunday
dinner that he should be invited to it.   That it
was a pretty story anyway and carried her mind
back very vividly to the charm of her childhood
home as she remembered it.

I also was introduced to a Mrs. Henry
Packman, a sister-in-law to Mrs. Emma Packman
who also came from the same locality and who
also had met Mr. Dickens there.   Between them
I was corrected somewhat as to my memory of
the geography of the neighborhood.

CHAPTER XXIX

At breakfast next morning we discovered that the artist had planned to end his visit that day but our host pursuaded him to remain at least another day as he wanted, he said, to take him to Wyngham Well, where he would show him a picture that would delight him. The name of this place, Wyngham Well, immediately excited my attention.

Forgetting myself, I blurted out, "That's where my grandmum lives, sir!"

But I quailed remorsefully when the master turned to me and sternly said, "Yes, I know it is," in a tone that was a rebuke for my temerity.

As we left the table to go outside, as usual Edward pleaded to be taken along with them. In my heart I hoped he would win the privilege even though I felt myself in too much disgrace to be invited. But instead, there seemed some logical reason why Edward should not go and to this he assented with lovely grace as he always did. (The children of this home were guarded well and their best interests looked after, but I did not observe so much of petting toward them as was customary even in my own home.)

We boys had followed the gentlemen outside and the weather was lovely and mild.   Edward was sent to the stables with some message
for Ted and then the master addressed me,
pointing to the Mastiff Rondo.   "See; Rondo
seems ill, look at him, poor fellow; take him
down the road a bit, Billy, to the end of our
fence, and just around the corner by the little
gate you'll find a bed of marsh mallow; coax him
to eat some of it; lots of it, it will do him good."

Well, I hadn't noticed anything wrong with
Rondo.   I had been romping with him before
breakfast and he was now watchfully waiting for
me to resume the pastime.   Then at my whistle
and his lumbering response, Mr. Dickens called
sharply to him "here!"

Looking me over, he added, "It's damp
down there, get your coat and hat on," and as
though to impress me with his command, he repeated, "Make him eat it, stuff him with it!"

He then continued on toward the pergola
with his pipe, laughing, accompanied by the
artist with his pipe, also laughing while I found
myself suddenly promoted to a great responsibility as veterinarian and nurse to Rondo, who
to me did not appear very ill but instead over-
joyed at being let out of the grounds.

I hadn't the slighest idea as to what marsh
mallow was, what it looked like, what ailment it
cured or what its pharmaceutical property might
be, but as I was told there was a bed of it around
the corner and near the gate there could be no
trouble finding it.   On arrival I found a dozen

things that might be it and then again might be
the very opposite, and poisonous. But I tried
them all from tree leaves to lichens, tasting
them, as though that would help me any. I argued with Rondo, who was as busy sniffing
around as I was, that he ought to know for himself what was good for him. At last I found
something that had a familiar taste and that was
somewhat palatable, so, setting the example for
the dog I ate of it, and the dog ate of it because
I ate and because I stuffed it in his mouth. When
he seemed to tire of this pursuasion, I turned
him on his back and sitting on him myself, I was
busy stuffing it in and he, spitting it out and
getting disgusted with that sort of play, when carriage with two gentlemen came along and stopped.

        "Well, how are you getting along?" called
Mr. Dickens.

        And I told him, "I don't know how much
he has swallowed, sir, but I have stuffed plenty
of it in."

        I had been commiserating with Rondo this
half hour on being ill because the master had
said he was and in spite of my own judgment that
there was nothing the matter with him and it
seemed heartless and quite out of place for them
to make such uproarious fun of it as they were
doing, Ted, with a broad grin on his face, pretended to be having difficulty in holding the res-
tive horses who were whinneying their laughter
too. Then when Mr. Dickens descended and got
a duster from Ted and went over me with it, in
my zeal as a nurse I had become very weedy and
dusty, and then opened the little gate and coaxed

the dog through it with a good-bye to him, and
then coaxed me up beside Ted who was trying in
a very silly way to keep his face straight. After
all this, I was open-mouthed with wonder. What
was going on?

The horses, rested for a week, were so
straining to be off that I could not take my eyes
off them and I was in such a muddle myself that
I scarcely breathed.

After passing the village Ted asked the
master, "Which woi, sir?"

The master replied, "Ask Billy, we're
going to his grandmother; he knows"

Oh! Rapture! I don't believe any sudden
announcement ever pleased or astonished me so
much in my life. I was quite beyond ability to
express it. At the risk of dislocating my neck
I turned quickly and stared back at the two gentlemen, who met my gaze stolidly but could not conceal the laughter in their eyes. I burst out with,
"Oh, my, I'm glad!" and in a fresh outburst,
"My! My! What would me mother say!"

"She knows!"

"She knows?" I cried in a puzzled tone.

"Yes! Yes!" And in a tone quite as
though it was a matter of indifference so far as
I ought to be concerned, Mr. Dickens added,
"Yes, I saw your parents the other day; don't
bother <u>me</u> now! You show Ted the way."

I suppose the horses had been steadily
trotting forward the last half minute or so but
for me the world had stopped, then turned upside down, then right side up, as it did when I
cartwheeled. But as soon as my eyes would
focus I turned to the horses' ears again and
found them bobbing up and down, up and down,
as before, to the rhythm of their pacing hoofs.

I heard Ted's gruff, "Wull, laad, w'ich
woi be ut?"

The question seemed stupid. All hands
knew how green I was to the country and to the
roads; but as I looked up at Ted and started to
answer, I caught his sly quizzical glance and realized they were all chaffing me and so I pertly
said, "Oh, you know all right, all right!" and
then got busy thinking it all out. It was a poser
and Mr. Dickens had just told me not to bother
him. So I pondered.

Mr. Dickens had gone according to his
own announcement on an unavoidable journey just
when, naturally, he would have preferred to remain to entertain his guest and as a makeshift
he had commissioned me to take his place as
guide and scout. The guest, taciturn and unin-
teresting to me at first, had in three days
changed his demeanor while our host was absent
so that we were now chummy friends.

On Mr. Dickens' return, and evidently
overnight, this trip to Wyngham had been cooked
up between the men. Early that morning both of
them had been to the stables; had sent to the

meadows for the horses; had instructed Ted and had taken him into their kidnapping conspiracy. They had conceived that casual announcement at the table and had anticipated my excitement over it. They had purposely squelched me, and they had sent Edward away while they fooled me to fool the dog. They had ordered me to get my hat and coat (which was not at all necessary in treating the dog) and they had sent me not up but down the road, the better to be picked up without observation at the house.

Oh! there was a conspiracy sure and Ted was in on it. I had already learned to know that fellow; that last glance I had picked up made me sure there was something up. But what was it? Why the mystery? Mr. Dickens had seen my parents "the other day" but where? Why, at my home of course, and in the evening of course, else he would not have met Father. Had he planned to see them? Why? What for? Why hadn't he given me the opportunity to send along a message?

In attempting to piece this out another mystery crept in: I suddenly remembered that message from Father to Mr. Elliot. It had been written and posted on the evening of the day our host left home. I had not mentioned the man's name in my letters to my mother; I had referred to him only as the florist, the daddy of the gate-keeper. How did father know his name was Elliot? Why, from Mr. Dickens, of course. But what connection was there between Dickens and Father and bulbs and Elliot and Wyngham--oh, I had to resolutely put it away. It's just some plot he's working out for a story.

Besides, this pondering interfered with my
contemplation of the rhythmic bobbing of two
pairs of ears and the enjoyment of very beautiful
scenery which had now changed from architectural
exhibits of mansions with wonderful doorways and
walls, queer arches and queerer gates, and hedges
cut with geometrical designs or trimmed here as
a huge elephant and there as a rhinoceros under
which one went as through an arch or as a portcullis, under which a child would dodge with fear
and trembling--changed now to big houses with
scores of gables all different, each pointing to
its own particular cardinal point of the compass,
and with a quantity of immature gables between
them looking as though they had been arrested in
their growth when they found that there were no
more cardinal points of the compass to point to
and had scorned intermediate ones, and churches
with towers like fortresses that didn't seem holy
and others with minarets and steeples which did.

And the streets had changed from hard
macadam that gave back a click-er-ti-clack from
shod hoofs to the thud-thud-thud of soft turf
roads.   And the verdure had changed from towering elms which vines clambered up and around,
to cypress-trimmed windbreaks, to here and there
some oak woods and thickets of shrubbery. There
were hedges enclosing dairy farms and sheep
pastures and milch cows, and there were stone
walls, usually of cobble but sometimes of huge
chalk blocks of irregular shapes, that enclosed
swine yards and sheep folds.

The whole aspect of the country then was
a rolling undulating surface resembling the swell-
ing ocean.   It was the corn field, the browsing

ground for the famous Kentish mutton sheep, the
range for the shepherd with the crook, the paradise of England.

The thudding hooves took us past the stub-
bled fields with here and there a string of women
and children gleaning, heaps of straw thrashed,
stacks of corn in the straw waiting to be thrashed,
the thrashers at work here and there throwing
dust into the air, and all the while the drone of
machinery seemed to mutter requiems for the
old flail. From the furnace a thin column of
smoke that tried to go straight up but was caught
by the draft from the fans and twisted and lost
itself in the swirling dust seemed like a funeral
pyre for the old, old scythe.

Ted evidently knew the proper direction
to take, all right, all right, and we bowled along
it at a merry pace; the ground was damp from
the humid air, and yielding to the horses' feet;
meadow larks and thrushes warbled welcome or
screamed derision at us.

I know only the general direction we took
but not the exact location of Wyngham Well. It
was not on the most traveled highway to coastal
ports and pleasure resorts but lay somewhere between them, hidden away in the chalky terrain
like a deep saucer with a roughly serrated edge
with towering old elms and beeches about, giving
the deep swale the appearance of having an ochre-
colored ruching collar. One would not find the
vale unless carefully directed to it. As its village
name implies, it was a hole in the ground at the
bottom of which was a large pond, many acres in

extent and fed by everlasing springs of intense
coldness from out of the chalk strata drainage of
the uplands in which it lay.   The thin lane leading down into it, not noticable but for the trail
leading to it from the hard moors, was steep and
damp and craggy, moss and clinging ferns crawled
everywhere on the rocks and trunks of the trees
that overhung the lane.   A single tiny rivulet
entirely concealed by shrubbery received the overflow from the pond and carried it through a narrow cleft in the yellow mellowed chalk to somewhere in the south where it disappeared in the
rock strata.

Although the high nasal tones of ten thousand tongues and throats of as many hucksters in
as many different localities of London yell " 'Ere's
ya Wyngham Well watercress!   'ere's ya Wyngham
Well watercress," from six to eight o'clock every
morning of the year and have been doing so for
centuries, and, no matter the nationalities and
languages of these ten thousand tongues and throats,
every yeller used the same slogan and the same
tone (except some say "watercresses") for they
have inherited the cry if they be natives and they
have scrupulously learned its tone and the formula, if they be alien.   It was the sound rather than
the words which indicated the trade call and its
significance was understood by steady patrons long
before the words were distinguished.   Watercress
was a staple commodity of London.   It graced,
and gave a touch of color and fragrance to, every
meal and was indispensible at tea with thin bread
and butter, hot muffins, and shrimps or peri-
winkles.

But of all the millions that patronized the
hucksters--and the hucksters themselves--I doubt
if there were one in a hundred thousand who
knew where Wyngham Well is.   I think rather
it was accepted as the botanical name of the plant.

CHAPTER XXX

And yet, the little place which had not
fifty permanent inhabitants and not more than a
dozen homes and not one of these observable
each from the others because of the intervening
foliage, was so rife with history and with myth
that any one of the old heads of the very old
families there could recite it for hours wonderfully delightfully, if one could but understand his
idiom.

The particular home that I was seeking,
or, that our party was seeking, was that of my
maternal grandparents. It had to be inquired
after, which was linguistically easy for Ted, as I
had not seen it myself since I was five. The place
had been graphically described by my parents to
Mr. Dickens only a few evenings prior, and by
him to the artist only last evening and this jolly
trip was the outcome of it. Both stories must
have been picturesquely told; first by my parents
to have induced Mr. Dickens to take a day off to
verify it, and second, by Mr. Dickens himself to
have induced the artist to abandon his former
plans to come visit and sketch it.

I do not suppose the journey was made
simply to meet a couple of old, small, and lonesome people who were fine examples of English

peasantry and whose ancestry for many centuries
had been peasants, nor was it to deplore with
them the fact that with their demise the name
and the race of "Ghennett" from the Year One
(the name Anglicised from the Druidic to "Ken-
nett") would expire and with it would expire the
last of the shepherds with a crook; nor to hear
from them that their family of seven had mostly
either passed on or were scattered to India and
Australia among the nation's defenders and the
remnant were getting ready for America. Nor
had we come to be shown the centuries-old loom
that had woven the shepherd garment of fustian
(not the fustian of the present which is of cotton
and flax but the fustian of their ancestry back to
the time of the first loom, which was flax and
wool, as made before cotton and America were
discovered) which consisted of a body shirt of
blue linen, trousers of fustian to the knee with
buckles of bone which buttoned at the side and
hung at the waist of the shirt, over this a double-
breasted waist-coat that was indeed double-breasted
and reached nearly to the knees, over these a
smock that reached from neck to the ankles, very
loose, buttoned all the way up the back with home-
made hard-wood buttons the size of a crown and
with big paunch pockets under each arm, each
large enough to carry a sick lamb or if lucky
enough a hare or two, if poaching were good, a
sou'wester made of the same material but doubly
thick and oiled for hot summer and rainy day use,
and the weasel-skin cap, fur inside and out, that
hung down below the collar and covered the ears,
for winds.

No, the journey was not made for any of
this but to get a sketch for a picture of one of

the oldest thatched cottages in England, one that
had been thatched over and over again, but at
decades intervals, until the covering was now
several feet thick.

        We were met with a stolid, almost word-
less, but pathetic welcome by my old grandfather
and by my trembling, mumbling (because she was
toothless) grandmother, who was inarticulate with
joy and almost sightless from tears, hugging and
patting her favorite grandchild.

        But we were looked for and expected be-
cause (as it turned out) Father had dispatched a
message to them, saying I would come that day
in a carriage, and also, as they understood it
"with a nobleman." Only a few hours prior had
they read the letter. Through tears and failing
eyes, how pathetically they tried to discern the
features of the "nobleman," of both "noblemen"
as they were presented by me in turn.

        Almost immediately after our arrival,
Granny reached down a jerked hare from the
rafters, green with mellowing age, and prepared
its cooking with an abundance of garden, orchard,
and berry stores. It made a goodly spread and
we city folk had a toothsome dinner. Ted, who
had now put the horses to their food, had then
been followed around by a lot of young un's who
had no difficulty in understanding and being understood in their dialect, and now sat at the same
table with the "noblemen" and received the same
deference from the old folks.

        Mr. Dickens and the artist drank in every-
thing as they drank in Granny's mulberry wine

and O'd and A'd a good bit over both, and then
they had separated, the artist to work ecstatically
while daylight lasted.   Work he did, between bites
of pork turn-overs made from the chitterlings of
home-grown pigs, and raspberry tarts and drinks
of rich, cold milk, and then blackberry wine and
temptings of russet-brown-pippins, and big, red,
hairy gooseberries, each of which I silently
slipped to his elbow.

And the nobleman-reporter, with those
long strides of his, walked entirely around the
vale and around the pond, which to me looked
more like an emerald green carpet than a body
of water and just the place to cartwheel on. He
met the manager of the watercress industry, from
a near-by village on the moor, who with his fifty
men scientifically cultivated the cress so that it
was wholesome the year around.   Mr. Dickens
got from him much commercial information regarding it: of its small-leaved, tender, pale-green
offerings in early spring when it was most delicious and expensive; of its abundance and cheap-
ness and popularity in the lush time of the early
summer; of its dark-green color and larger leaf
and thicker stem as it approached bloom and was
prevented from blooming by constant pruning and
thinning; of its old age in the winter when its
green was merged to a bronze brown and when
its taste was sharper and more rank but again
very popular.   He was told the intensive culture
it required to prevent watercress from running
lush and wild in the autumn and thus being ruined.

And then the nobleman returned to the
artist to report that Wyngham Well was a veri-
table paradise.   He avouched it was a pity they

could not remain longer.   The artist agreed with
him and I agreed heartily with both.

Ted had been busy helping with old un's to
end the dinner and he had been entertaining them
and me with folk-lore of the vale and of its old
inhabitants, tales he interleaved with sly banter
about me and my awful doin's.   As we soon had
to leave, he carried to the coach a hamper of
goodies that was to be forwarded to Mother and
another for the nobleman's lady with Granny's respectful wishes for "M'lady's 'appiness" and still
another for Ted himself and his "good wife."

Then as the sun was getting ready to drop
over the rim of the saucer and Ted had the team
ready and champing to be off, and the artist had
given a last survey of his work, in the rough
more comprehensible to him than to us, and the
last trembling good-byes were called from the
old folks, we were off.   But it was a little hard
for me to break away, for young as I was I
didn't like Granny's wan looks and the pathetic
droop of her body, and I had not penetrated the
ox-like reserve of Grand-dad, I had quite an inclination for a cry, but...

Well, the horses had quite a pull up that
long, steep hill but they were fresh and eager
and made no trouble of getting us back to Gad's
Hill before midnight; a wonderful day for all of us.

As we entered the house Mr. Dickens bent
to me and in the most tender voice he had ever
addressed me with, quietly asked, "Have you enjoyed the day, Willie?"

The only reply I could trust myself to make was throwing my arms around his legs and burying my head in his tummy.

Late as it was that night I pondered quite a while before finally saying the pretty thought I like to sleep with. The mysteries of the trip were unravelling but I concluded they would not be solved until I got back to London. Why had we gone so suddenly to Wyngham? Why could I not have dressed up in the velvets to show off-- instead of in my common hiking clothes? That would have been jolly romantic indeed.

There was no prior concert about lying abed the next morning after our return from Wyngham Well but it is a fact that we did not have our sun-up walk. The artist went to Cobham Hall to square himself for avoiding it the day before and to get some sketches before he was to return to London. I am sorry I cannot remember the name of this artist. I seem to feel sure that he was a Belgian and the name "Bluhardt" comes to me confusedly from my deep-most brain. I did not find out what became of his pictures; I suppose Mr. Dickens got some of them. Where, especially, went the "Gates Ajar?"

CHAPTER XXXI

I remember well one evening by the fire-place in the drawing room, with my host sitting on the fireside nearest the portico entrance conversing with Aunt Georgy opposite him with a work-basket in her lap, and Dora and Henry working at their school lessons. These two were standing against, lolling upon, a large oval center table under a heavy chandelier with cut-glass pendants encircling a large glass oil lamp with reflector which pulled up and down by counter-poised weights. Edward and I were on the floor between the table and the hearth playing some game, I cannot remember what. Evidently we disturbed Henry at his work. Reaching back his foot without looking around he caught me in the face with it with force sufficient to topple me over against his father's chair. Without leaving his chair, Mr. Dickens picked me up and held me up and held me there with his arm around me while the lady and Edward did some scolding at Henry. Henry expressed some contrition for his violence and I might never have remembered the incident again except that while holding me Mr. Dickens asked me if I didn't feel like swearing.

"Oh, no, sir; I know he didn't mean to and besides it didn't hurt much."

"Well, I know you don't swear at home,

Willie, but how about slum swearing? Didn't you
have some of that in mind, eh?"

"Oh, you must mean "K Cab G Nals," I
told him.

"What kind of swearing is that?" Mr.
Dickens pretended to look shocked.

"That isn't swearing at all, sir; that's
'back slang,' sir; what the mugs call 'thieves'
Latin', sir." And I explained how the term "back
slang," if spoken backward itself, would have to
make four syllables: "Kay cab gee nals."

He repeated this over and over, awkwardly
I thought, and then asked, "But if you wanted to
swear, if you wanted to say, 'go to the devil,'
how would you say that?"

Before I could answer Aunt Georgia hur-
riedly exclaimed, "Oh! Charles! You shouldn't
ask him such a thing as that."

"All right," he admitted, "but how about
'go to Jericho'?"

This didn't sound so bad in company, but
I looked inquiringly at the mistress who seemed
doubtful but did not protest. I answered him,
" 'Og ot reg e oc,' sir," but quickly added, "oh,
but they don't say 'reg e oc,' sir, they say 'le'."

While he was puzzling this out, Edward,
who was paying intense attention to this instruction, as indeed were the other two members of
the family, held up something we had been playing

with and asked, "What do you call this in that
language?"

In the same reproving tone his father
might have used, I told him, "That's 're ven d
nim'; that means 'never mind'." I explained that
"k cab g nals" was very limited in vocabulary
and was only used mixed in with proper talk or
with common slang in such way that a listener--
like a "peeler" or P C man, or a warden, would
be puzzled in understanding it even though it were
directed to himself. There were printed text
books for it in the slums and there even were
schools that taught it, especially in Seven Dials,
where they also taught dip work, and that the
codes were known as "pid klat." I told them
that brother Fred had got hold of one of these
text books and copied it and he and I had studied
it together and were tolerably proficient. The
police tried to learn it in order to understand
confidences between suspects and prisoners, but
were largely unsuccessful. I gave some examples
of it which were quite bewildering to them, as it
was intended to be to the officers.

Many years afterwards when brother Fred
and I were in business together in America we
often used 'g nals' to put over some information
not intended for listening ears, pretending it was
Gaelic, and got away with the deception. We
argued to ourselves that there was no more im-
propriety in doing this than for book writers to
insert words and phrases in French or Latin in
their writing, knowing the most of their readers
would not understand it.

There seems to be a common belief that
in writing David Copperfield Dickens intended to
portray some of the story of his own life.   This
impression must have gained some hold with me
as a child for once when the master was conver-
sationally inclined and was quizzing me about this
and that, I asked him if it were true.

We were seated in a shady place by the
roadside on my account, for rest, he must have
noticed my difficulty in keeping up with his pace,
and I had been telling him of some searches I
had made in the area to locate the scenes in the
opening chapter of Great Expectations and that I
thought I had found some of them, particularly the
graveyard, but that I had not found Joe's Forge.

"That was a long time ago, you know,
Billy, perhaps it is not there now."

Something prompted me to blurt out, "Is
it true, sir, that you are David Copperfield?"
and I looked at him very earnestly as I asked.
He was slow to answer.   He first looked at me
steadily, then shifted his gaze across the road
but without seeing anything and after a long pause
and without again meeting my eyes, he rose,
drawing me up with him as much as to say well
we're rested, let's get along, but the words he
uttered were, "Some people say I am, don't they
Billy?"

That's as far as I got on that subject and
I was disappointed; but I seem to remember that
there was a note of sadness in his voice as he
said this.

On another occasion with the family assembled, and Mr. Dickens at the fireside as
previously depicted, there came a rat-a-tat-tat
at the knocker of the door and one of the children
started to answer it.

The master said, "Here, I'll go," and
opened the door, stepped outside, and drew the
door closed and we heard but could not disting-
uish some conversation. In a minute or two the
master returned, followed by a gentleman, and
they crossed the room diagonally to Mr. Dickens'
library while the gentleman observed the lady and
made a sidewise bow of recognition to her but did not
speak. We heard faintly what must have been a
heated discussion within, which lasted for some
time, even continuing as they returned through the
living room and back out the front door.

On the master's return to his chair, apparently vexed, Aunt Georgy asked him, "What's
the matter with him now, Charles?"

"Oh, he insists he must sign that last
sketch before it goes to the engraver, and I
won't allow it."

"But, Charles," said the lady in a questioning rather than argumentative tone, and molli-
fyingly, "he drew it, didn't he?"

"Yes, yes, but I'm buying his services,
not his name, and I won't have his name on it."

I can distinctly recall the appearance of
that gentleman illustrator as he crossed the room
both ways. He was about the same age and about

the same height as Mr. Dickens, though not so
erect, in fact a little stoop-shouldered with his
head pushed slightly forward as though forcing
the lead; a little bald in front and with rather long
and heavy hair behind. He had no beard. His
arms seemed long but this may have been because
of his drooping shoulders. He carried a flat
portfolio under his arm and had no cane (which
gentleman usually carried) nor hat (perhaps he
had left these outside). I have never seen portraits of the illustrious illustrators of the master's works but I have heard that they were
mostly temperamental people, as I think I would
be if I could do half as well. Perhaps I would
recognize "Phiz" if I were to see his portrait.

During my association with Mr. Dickens
I had been impressed with his extraordinary keen-
ness of observation. He seemed to see all of
everything his eyes lit upon and not simply de-
tailed parts. As a child, I felt that there was
no use in trying to deceive him, even in fun, or
of concealing from him any part of my mind: he
had a way of getting it; all of it. He was a mind-
reader. In remembering the above incident, I
now can see that in trying to get the necessary
detail in any of his illustrations that would bring
to another's understanding that which he had himself created in his text, he would encounter difficulty, especially with any kind of professional and
temperamental illustrator who would presume to
interpret the text differently. I'm sure too that
Mr. Dickens had a frequent fervent wish that he
might be independent of the skilled fingers of the
artist. It is known that Dickens was often in hot
water with his artists and had been known to express a wish for the skill to do his own illustra-

tions independently of them.   To some extent he
did practice for it but it wasn't in him.   He had
an independent spirit; but I would not have one
think he felt independent of his fellow men, except that (of course with some exceptions) he
used them, including his artists, as vehicles, like
the prototypes "his boys," with which to vivify
his imaginative and creative genius.

CHAPTER XXXII

My visit to Gad's Hill ended very happily on the following Saturday after breakfast. Mr. Dickens had gone to London the day before and Ted was to take Edward and me in and bring the master back.

I had brought down my little blue box with its romantic contents, used but once but with several purposes, and I had been to the rear to thank Ruth and to leave a crown on the sideboard for the many nice little things she had done for me and she had told me to see her again before we drove off. So when Ted drove up and was ready, I shook hands with Dora and Henry who were kind enough to say they had enjoyed my visit and hoped I was pleased with it too. And I did my best to impress my gratitude on Miss Georgina for her hospitality and care. Then I returned to Ruth who kissed me good-bye much as she would a little brother and placed in my hands a beautifully made-up nosegay, wet with dew, with the stems packed in moss and wrapped with tissue: as artistically fashioned as though by an experienced floral artist. I was very much surprised at this fragrant gift and quite overcome with its magnificence and I started to stammer a fresh volume of thanks to Ruth.

She cut in loftily, and quite as though she washed her hands of such a fragrant responsibility said, "Oh, don't thank me, that coomed from the Lodge a few minutes ago."

"Oh, oh," I managed to exclaim, quite out of breath with ecstacy, "Who brought it? Emma? Eh?" knowing very well it must have been she or at least that she had had a hand in it--perhaps sent it by the young un's.

"The idea!" said Ruth, "The idea! You conceited fop, no. It wa'nt your pretty gate-keeper 'tall, it was, er, the master's Woodland Maid done it."

"Oh, but then it's for the Master!" I cried, with a note of disappointment I ought to have been ashamed of.

"Oh, no; it's for your mother with her father's respecks," said Ruth teasingly.

"That's fine!" I shouted "I am almost as pleased as if they were intended for myself! When you see her again give her this for me!" I threw my arms around Ruth with a good hug, except for the care I was giving to the flowers in my hands, and gave her a smack that could be heard all the way to the Lodge and happily ran to the front much flustered.

I carried the bouquet out front and it was much admired by the family and it reminded me to specially thank Miss Georgina for the very pretty flowers that had appeared every day in my room. This seemed to puzzle her a bit, until

she caught Ruth's face which had followed me
through the house.

To Ruth she said laughingly, "So, so!
you've been doing your little bit, too, have you?"

Ruth, pointing to the nosegay in my hand,
said, "Thoi coomed from the soime ploice as
that un', mum."

I afterward learned that our maid Ruth
had been a base traitor to my confidences. She
had quickly visited the Lodge after that threat
that she had better "look into that 'maid' business
for herself." There she had ingratiated herself
with the little gate-keeper and the gate-keeper had
learned from her all about the "little lord's" costume and his first appearance in it. The gate-
keeper had later visited Ruth, in Ruth's own
room adjoining mine. Being then in such close
proximity to the little lord's costume, her curiosity had lead to the exhibition of it. In short,
the gate-keeper now knew as much as our maid
knew.

Also it was the little gate-keeper that had
brought the nosegay which she had made up herself under her father's direction; she had been
concealed in the kitchen when the nosegay was
given to me and had heard all that was said and
seen all that was done. It was enough to shake
my confidence in women. But Mother got the
nosegay all right and with the respects of Mr.
Elliot, too.

Soon goodbyes were over and Ted, the
coachman, and my dear friend Edward Dickens

and I climbed up into the coach and we trotted
and rattled out of the drive, me waving and Ruth
waving back, and me happy for yet another journey but sad to be leaving.

On the way to the city we passed through
the pretty village of Chalk, which in my rambling
I had visited before, and there Ted and Edward
both noticed and seemed interested in a pony attached to a chaise with no one in it which was
standing before a neat little cottage. The fact
that no one was in the chaise is what was impressive to Ted, so much so that he halted,
looked around and up and down, and then passing
the lines to me, got down and went to the house
and used the knocker until a maid came. Thereupon something was said, the maid disappeared,
and very quickly a nice, rosy-cheeked, white-
haired old gentleman took her place. Ted, quite
unlike himself, to this gentleman made some
voluble remarks with ample gesticulation, then,
both of them came down the walk looking all
around and up and down the village road, while
the old gentleman, who was lame with one leg
and wore a steel support for it, seemed much exasperated over something and got quite red in the
face. Then Ted seemed to be consulted about
something that had the effect of bringing their
glances over to our barouche, even centering, it
seemed, on me. I was presently an object of
scrutiny and appraisal. The only thing Edward
and I heard said, as Ted started to leave, was:

"I wish you would, Ted, it won't be much
out of your way, you know."

"Not a bit, Doctor," Ted answered.

"All right, then," said the nice old gentle-man, revealed to me as a doctor, "I'll be home before you get there."

And at that Ted mounted, took the lines from me and drove off while the doctor shouted "Whoa! Whoa there! Whoa!" to the eager pony hitched to his own chaise which showed an incli-nation to follow us.

I had been sitting back with Edward until Ted had called me to take the lines and I now started to climb back to him but Ted laid a de-taining hand on me and, turning to Edward, said, "Bide a bit, young master, ar warn't to gab a mite wi' Billy, eh!"

This seemed all right with the young master. Ted, after looking at nothing for a few minutes, impressively began, "Oo sees thet shay?" pointing backward with his whip without looking around.

"Yes," I answered, curious. I had wondered intensely during his reverie what the "gab" was to be about.

"Oo sees thur wuz no boi a 'old'n on ter tha lines?"

"Yes."

"Oo sees an' oo 'ears 'ow the doctor said 'Whoa'?"

"Yes," I said, trying to get the drift, "yes, I heard him."

"Sposen the doctor ba' int by an' noobody ba'int by to soi 'Whoa,' tha nag 'ud a run, 'udn't 'e?"

It looked likely to me that he would and I said so.

"Wull, wur wuz tha boi?"

This was asked in a tone that indicated that being a boy myself I certainly ought to know. But not having the wisdom to think it out and yet unwilling to admit the deficiency I parried. "How should I know, Ted?"

This admission of my lack of discernment gave Ted the opportunity, which he seized, to prove the superiority of his own. "Wull, 'ow aboot thet sweet shop we sees a coom'n tru' tha willage?--ya sees thet din't ya?" taking for granted I suppose that all boys see sweet shops.

"Yes, I saw that," I admitted, "what of it?" although I began dimly to see what the coach-man was driving at.

"Wull, ya sees the felle wi' the cock 'at on an' wi' tha featha' in ut, in thur, din't ya?" And without waiting for me to admit that come to think about it I had seen such a fellow, he added, "Wull! That's 'e, und it's tha larst o' 'e, too; Doctor Hanlan 'as 'ad enow o' 'e!"

"Will he lose his place, d'ye think, Ted?" I asked, trying solicitously to carry water on both shoulders by sympathizing first with the doc-tor and then with the groom who was in danger

of losing his cocked hat and feather. As Ted
seemed slowly ruminating over what he really did
think, I urged him again, "Will he, d'ye think,
Ted?"

Not having come to a conclusion as to
what he thought and seemingly in need of more
tangible evidence on which to base his belief as
to what would happen, Ted glanced quizzically
down at me.

"Wut 'ud oo a dun if oo 'ud be a 'old'n
'o tha lines?"

Disregarding my own question and lapsing
myself into the vernacular, I shouted, "I'd be a
'oldin' on ter 'em, of course!" and then grasping his meaning better, I added, "I wager ya, I
'oodn't drop 'em an' roon away to a sweet shop,
Ted."

"Ay," said Ted, slowly nodding his head,
positive again his own opinion would not admit of
dispute, "ay, thet's jus' what ar toled un."

Then as if to forestall any further questioning as to whom "un" referred to and having
now done, for him, a day's work of talking and
thinking, he straightened himself into a coachman's attitude, grasped the lines closer, held his
hands farther apart, looked straight ahead, chir-
rup't to the horses that had been taking advantage
of his preoccupation, and ended the subject, my
twice repeated question still unanswered. So I
climbed over to my companion to enjoy the remainder of the journey and with a regretful feeling
that I was so soon to part from him.

I ask pardon, dear reader, for inflicting
this bit of Kent dialect. I know the sound of it
very well myself and I have carefully spelled it
out for you but I fear you may have had difficulty
in following it. Not all Kentish people spoke so
broadly as Ted but it was the common idiom of
provincial and isolated spots such as Wyngham
Well. Its derivation is entirely Briton or Saxon
and not at all intermixed with continental languages, even though it is in close aural proximity with some of them. Mr. Dickens himself
was quite familiar with it and besides he had
Ted's brogue as a constant reminder. The
master could on occasion speak it very well and
often put it into ordinary conversation, so of
course he could write it, but he modified it very
much when making his characters speak it, such
as Joe Gargery.

The artist had hardly understood a word
of it although he enjoyed listening to it and he
averred that except when it was spoken with a
gutteral delivery, it sounded soft and rounded and
euphonious. It was always spoken slowly and deliberately but from a limited vocabulary and with
almost no flexing of the face muscles. One un-
accustomed to it had to rely much on the eye of
the speaker or on foreknowledge of the subject
matter to determine a fair meaning of it. It is
English "as she was spoke," long, long before
Shakespeare.

CHAPTER XXXIII

I arrived home feeling as though I had made a trip around the world. Feeling too as though the slums of London and the habits of it and the idiom of it and the wickedness of it and the squalor of it were things I had experienced in some former existence and that I was now reborn to another, cleaner, brighter--a happier world.

I marvel now that with so few object lessons of correct deportment before me and so many in my slum associations that were crude, still I managed to conduct myself at Gad's Hill in such a way as to overcome the preconceived and unfavorable impression under which I was first received and to leave its family giving such a show of confidence and regret at my departure. And I am quite sure that the influence of that family, coming as it did at that exact period of the formation of my character, had a wholesome effect upon all my subsequent conduct in life.

Also I am sure that while Magdalen Ragged School gave me a better foundation in the 3 R's than my older brothers and sisters had attained at the parochials, that it was more the unostentatious, almost unspoken spur of Mr. Dickens' faith in my ability to rise, that enabled me to pull myself up by my own boot-straps.

The supineness that had made me content
with things as they were had given place with
my stay at Gad's Hill to such an exaltation as
Pip, in whose very footsteps I had been treading,
must have had.   In contemplation of his "great
expectations" he had sworn "No more wet grounds,
no more dykes and sluices..."   Only, I substituted America and Opportunity for his London
and Estrella.

My letters to the family must have been
very deficient in recording and describing events,
for it took days and days to amplify them with
verbal details.   The nosegay for mother was the
very first she had ever received from anyone
outside of the family, and of course it centered
much of her inquiries on the donor and thus
brought about many expressions of gratitude toward him (I gave her Ruth's interpretation of
who the donor was) and cuddling for me.

"Father must certainly write to him our
thanks," she said.   It ran through my mind that
that might complicate things a bit.

And to my inquiry as to how they got the
name of Elliot they explained that on Mr. Dickens'
last visit they had shown him the letter from
Utah and the sego lily bulbs and the 'hoppers had
eaten everything above ground, and how because
of this the government had then made it the state
emblem.   Mr. Dickens had then suggested sending them to the florist of Cobham Park, whose
name was Thomas Elliot, and whom I had met.
And this entailed the story of the Lodge gate and

of its keeper, which Mr. Dickens seems to have
told with some choice embellishments of his own,
and he told them something of how I was behav-
ing and to Mother's anxious inquiry as to the
velvet suit, he had some surprising things to say.
But the principal object of his visit, he had said,
was to tell them that he intended taking me on a
surprise visit to Wyngham to see my Granny and
he wanted to know how to find her and especially
to learn something about the history of the place
and of the ancestry of the old inhabitants there.
He said I had excited his curiosity as well as the
art instinct of a friend of his.   But he advised
that it might be best first to dispatch a line to
the old folks so that they would not be too greatly
agitated (how considerate this was); and of course
not to tell Billy as it would spoil his surprise
plans.

And father had sent such a dispatch that
very same night and had referred to Mr. Dickens
in it as a "noble gentleman" (naturally enough)
and this was interpreted by Granny as "nobleman"
(naturally enough, too).   And so the mystery of
it all turned out to be no mystery at all but just
a Dickens of a way to create intrigue.

With the sailing of the Amazon for
America, carrying off the firstborn, with his
earning capacity as a haberdasher and carrying
off the secondborn with her earning capacity as
a milliner, and both of them with a loving chum-
ship with the mother of necessity, came a re-
adjustment of affairs domestically.   We younger
ones had to step up a notch in responsibility.
The thirdborn gave up his job as engineer at the

kid-skin tannery and succeeded to the place made
vacant by the firstborn at the haberdashery in
the Borough.

My own position as fourth-born improved
by a recommendation of Mr. Dickens, seconded
by Ted, which promoted me to a position as
groom and lackey to the chaise and pony of Dr.
Hanlan, the nice old gentleman of the mysterious
conversation with Ted at Chalk. For that loqua-
cious fellow like his circumlocutionary master
had figured out in his own obtuse mind that Billy
would be needing a job after his holiday was over
at Gad's Hill. The negligent chaise boy at Chalk
had furnished Ted with an idea; the idea developed
as a supposition with his speech with the doctor;
it evolved from supposing to planning with his
next speech with his master; and it thereupon
turned into a letter from the master to me telling me to go apply for a job with his old friend
the doctor. Curiously enough, Dr. Hanlan had
been Mr. Dickens' own family physician when both
of them resided at Chalk during the master's
early married life.

I was to apply for the job at once and
alone, which I did, carrying with me a letter of
endorsement from my patron. This preliminary
visit brought a request that both of my parents
should return with me that evening. This was
attended to also and my qualifications were dis-
cussed--some of them at least (those pertaining
to cartwheeling, not being called for, were left
unrevealed).

It was asserted by both parents and con-
curred in by me, that even though I was not what

could be called an experienced groom, and knew
little of chaise or pony other than what I had
gained at Gad's Hill, I had learned a great deal
from Mr. Dickens' experienced coachman and
anyway I was quick at learning anything. As I
was not expected to drive and under no circum-
stance whatever to ride the pony, it required only
that if I could groom the pony and clean the stable
and keep my own room above the stable neat and
clean, and could wash and polish the chaise, and
clean windows and help the maid in the house;
and especially, if I could and would stay in the
chaise and hold the lines while the doctor was
busy with his patients (and here it was explained
that this was the nub of the rub, and the nub that
the last boy stumbled on); if all this, I would be
given a fair trial for a month and if the trial
warranted it, I would be engaged permanently at
twelve pounds and keep per year.

And so Ted's idea grew to fact.

I think it was my mother's charming wist-
fullness to get me safely into such a desirable
home and occupation, together with whatever my
patron's recommendation had been and whatever
Ted's conversation with him at Chalk had been,
that won me the decision. Together we visited
the coach-house and inspected my room, which
Mother was invited to rearrange as she pleased,
and then the pony, which was found to be a short,
thick-set fellow with roached mane and tail, that
Mother, who was the "horseman" of our family,
called a cob. He lazily resented being disturbed
from his beauty sleep and made to listen to his
good and his bad characteristics as related by
his master; and he evinced no desire to get ac-

quainted with a new groom, especially a slim
runt that didn't even know horse-talk.   Still he
seemed a good-natured fellow and indicated that
if we would let him alone now and let him sleep
while he had a chance--as he might be routed
out on real business at any minute--why, then,
he would see about me in the morning.

And by six o'clock next morning, nothing
untoward having disturbed his slumber, the pony
had that chance.   Instructed by the doctor, I was
doing my best to make him presentable to his
master's patrons.

I held that position for nearly a year and
was not once convicted of dropping the lines.
Better than this, I had won the confidence of that
dear old doctor and mistress who treated me
kindly and considerately; and I had become very
chummy with Martha, the maid; in fact I had
come to consider her, with possibly one exception, the very nicest maid in the world.

And as for the cob, well the cob had a
better reason for currying favor with me than I
had for currying him.   I was his god-father.
Learning that he had never had a cognomen--only
the appellation "animal," or "brute," or "beast,"
I consulted with the doctor and the mistress as
to the unseemliness of this and as to the necessity
of blessing him with a title of some kind, and as
I was the first to realize this propriety I was
given the privilege of being god-father to him.
I began planning for a suitable ceremonial for it
and was rather shocked a little later when the
doctor asked me to defer the event.   He thought
he could improve on my plans.   The question of

the name seemed at first not a weighty one, for
instantly my counterpart, Kit Nubbles came into
my mind and naturally this suggested the name
"Whiskers." But, I considered, perhaps Kit or
Mr. Dickens had a copyright on the name "Whiskers" and I didn't feel like stealing it. The next
alternative was a name that had a like ring to it,
and so "Blinkers" came in my mind. This name
seemed appropriate for a horse; even more so
than Whiskers; it sounded horsy. After two days
passed I was told that no improved name could be
thought of and I might proceed with the ceremony
at four in the afternoon.

I dreadfully wanted to invite some neighbor
boys not only as witnesses but to give the ceremony some distinction. I was told this was
strictly taboo but that Martha might assist if that
would do.

As the hour approached I considered the
form of my rites. The only christening I had
ever seen required taking the subject across the
arms and uttering a blessing ending with the
name. But Martha said she had seen it done by
sprinkling some drops of water on the head and
then pronouncing the name. So the maid's plan
was decided upon without a dissenting vote and I
brought the applicant out in the sunlight nicely
polished and be-ribboned and Martha came walking, ridiculously sanctimonious, from the house
(as though into a church) with the vessel of water,
holding it while I dipped in my fingers and
sprinkled the cob's head, acclaiming unctuously,
"By the authority vested in me I now name thee,
'Blinkers', amen."

And so the deed was done, Blinkers never knowing how perilously near, in my stage-fright, I had come to saying "Whiskers" instead of "Blinkers" and thus of ruining his career. Nor did I know until the ceremony was over that an audience of Mr. Dickens and Ted had been concealed in the vinery to witness it. Their inclusion had been the doctor's sly trick for these several days of putting me off. But Blinkers evidently appreciated this coming into a recognizable identity by ever afterward responding to orders when addressed. Strangely, too, in Spa Road and elsewhere from that day on I became "William" or "Reverend William," and "Billy" was no more.

That year for Blinkers was the most informative of any of the four years of his existence. At the end of it he knew most of all that I had ever known in my whole thirteen, for I had told it to him during the long waits at patients' houses and during my valet duties to him in his stall and during my serving duties to him at his meals. Because he did not interrupt me during these confidences by assuming to advise or suggest and because he was my only confidant and because he did not try to have the last word, or disagree with me, he got my sincere respect and my very solicitous attention. I have learned in my progress through life that this is the very best way to win respect and solicitous attention.

Blinkers showed he knew this by his fat sleek ribs and his bronze-brown hide and by his roached mane and his cropped and braided tail (tipped with a tress ribbon), and by his polished hoofs--one white and the others black; and he

showed it by his neighing welcome to me at my
first appearance in the morning and by his equine
osculation as I served his breakfast. And he
showed it by permitting my thorough domination
of him in matters of discipline. These develop-
ing virtues of Blinkers were noticed and acknowl-
edged by the doctor and brought some reflected
glory to me.

Also, and what was better, at this situation I had a lot of time for the study of good
books which I was permitted to select from a
well-stocked library, for there would be hours
and sometimes whole days when I would have nothing but routine duties. I had the opportunity of
listening in to good English conversation by intelligent people and because I must not, of course,
join in with them, I listened, but circumspectly,
all the more.

And Martha and I were well fed and ate
together and when there was much company,
which was only on anniversary occasions, the
mistress taught me to help the maid to serve.
And I was permitted one evening a week to visit
at home, which was not far away, and Mother or
any of my family were permitted to visit my
room. Mother often did, "to tidy it up a bit"
she said.

And so I wore the cocked hat with the
feather in it very jauntily and very happily and
the most instructive year of my life so far wore
away. I was weaned from piratin', I had improved
my language and my habits, and was now prepared for another step up. And the best of it
was that all of my twelve pounds went into the

emigration fund, bringing America that much
nearer.

There would be no need for me to enlarge
upon the events of this period but for some odd
coincidences which brought me back again to Mr.
Dickens. At that time I had a close familiarity
with Dickens' characters, most of them; with
their environment, their costumes, their dialect,
and their habits. And sometimes Mr. Dickens
talked about them with me.

On that picnic day I described, for instance, Mr. Dickens enjoyed himself in quizzing
us boys (we were all fairly familiar with his
stories) as to what they thought of this or that
character, his boy characters of course, and
why? Then he would single out a boy to answer,
much like a catachism in Sunday school. Later,
in my interview with him in the Coffee Shop and
at Gad's Hill and "Inspiration Point, " and in the
vestry at St. George the Martyr's Church in the
Borough, he indulged in this further. Especially
he drew from me which of his boy characters
interested me most and why? There wasn't much
hesitation for a reply, for of course it was Kit.
Kit Nubbles, in The Old Curiosity Shop. I knew
him like a book, I had got under his hide, into
his mind, and I had found many points of simi-
larity between us. True, Kit wasn't a cartwheeler and I resented a little that he had not
been given some physical trait of that kind instead of the master's giving it all to Tom Scott
whom I did not like!

("What! You don't like Tom Scott?--Why?"
asked Mr. Dickens.

("Why! Because he stuck to that horrible beast, Quilp, " said I.

("Yes, he was very faithful to his master, wasn't he?" said Mr. Dickens, reflectfully, "But don't you think that was more a merit than a fault?"

(I muttered something about, "I don't know about that, I wouldn't have had anything to do with the monster myself--that's all. "

(But it wasn't quite all for he had teasingly ended the subject for the time being with, "Oh, you're just jealous of Tom. " In the ensuing years I have played the characters of Daniel Quilp and Tom Scott and have enjoyed doing so.)

It was not in the direct line of traffic but it was almost as near for Ted to drive into the City by way of Spa Road as it was to go by Kent Road and Mr. Dickens would quite often pull up at the doctor's to speak to him (and give Ted a chance to bring ridiculous messages to me) and we compared notes and found that barring the piratin' 'abits of which I was now supposed to be weaned, in most points of resemblance I was really Kit the Second, and further, that our sweet little parlor maid, Martha, was really Barbara the Second; further, that dear, old, rosy-cheeked Mrs. Hanlan was really dear, old, rosy-cheeked Mrs. Garland the Second. Dr. Hanlan, lame with one leg so that walking was painful to him and the pony chaise a necessity, very fairly substituted for Mr. Garland, who was, the reader will remember, also lame with one leg; and last,

our four year old chaise pony so recently chris-
tened Blinkers had already in spite of his tender
years some of the tendencies of Mr. Garland's
chaise pony Whiskers, and could naturally be
Whiskers the Second.

So, imagination was now being verified
by fact.   Yet, after all, there is nothing strange
in this resemblance.   The counterpart of all of
the master's situations and of most of his characters exist throughout life, if we will but notice.
Weird tragedies are in the sordid corners of life;
hypocrisy and intrigue beckon in its smug deceit;
romance and adventure lie in the quest of it;
love and sacrifice both its penalty and reward.
For Dickens wrote only of conditions and of things
as they were, are, and perhaps always will be.
But, oh, how understandingly.

And so, another year wore away.

CHAPTER XXXIV

I have expressed myself as so contented
and happy in the home of Dr. Hanlan and of its
social advantages to me that my reasons for
leaving it require an explanation.

Six years before this our family firstborn,
Alfred Edwin, who was then thirteen, became the
shop-boy at the Haberdashery Establishment of
G. W. C. Cross, which was situated in the Borough or "Boro" as it was abbreviated, immediately opposite the Church of St. George the
Martyr. The haberdashery and its business had
come down by inheritance through many genera-
tions and "G. W. C.," as we all thought and
spoke of him, had been its owner since the as-
cension of Queen Victoria and he had also been
during all of this time the clerk of the parish.

At the time our firstborn entered the haberdashery there were there a Miss Esther
Cross, spinster, about forty-five, and a Mr.
William Cross, married, with two small children.
Brother and sister, these two, with the senior,
had operated the business as long as they could
remember. But about this time Mr. William
went into government--at Woolwich or Black-
pool--in some sort of naval office and our firstborn was supposed to be able feebly to succeed

251

him at least in the charman duties of the shop.
He was a handsome boy, my brother, tall for
his age, very studious, he grew up with the business and he grew in the esteem of G. W. C.,
and of Miss Esther. (As to the latter it was
saying a good deal, for Miss Esther was rarely
given to estimation.) Then the time arrived for
Alfred Edwin's emigration.

The essential requisites for this position,
stated in the order of their importance, were:
Absolute Honesty, Indefatigable Industry, and Unwavering Allegiance. These virtues the firstborn
had bestowed upon the Cross Haberdashery Establishment for six years.

During this time the Cross' senior and
daughter had become fairly intimate with our
parents and with all their progeny from the firstborn descending six steps to Polly the baby.
Having had such general satisfaction with the
firstborn and as his departure was positive and
imminent, it was proposed that the thirdborn,
Fred, fifteen, should succeed him as the haberdashery shop-boy. With two years more of age
at commencement of duties to begin with, and
with a broader knowledge of the business coached
into him by the retiring elder brother, Fred had
a good start and so for another year the thirdborn practiced the virtues of Absolute Honesty,
Indefatigable Industry, and Unwavering Allegiance,
together with the lesser, more numerous and decidedly more specific duties as a shop-boy. Then
his turn came to emigrate.

The second experiment having been as
successful as the first, it now came the turn of

the fourthborn to donate to Cross the several
virtues I have twice enumerated.   As father put
it, not regretfully however, "It's a case of breeding shop-boys for the Establishment of Cross. "
But Billy/William the Fourthborn had again to be
re-christened.   Thereafter I was "Harrison" to
avoid confusion with William Cross.

And had not British don't-care-ness and
British good-riddance-to-bad-rubbishness emptied
from its shores all of the remainder of the
family holus-bolus the following year, I suppose
the fifthborn, Harry, by then thirteen, would have
stepped into Harrison's shop-boy shoes, and
served his apprenticeship with these same virtues
and precisely these same duties, down to the
hanging of the very same broom on the very same
nail as during the past hundred years.

Now the good Dr. Hanlan and the sweet
Mistress Hanlan had known from the beginning all
about our impending emigration and that I was
taking the place as groom for only a year, as at
the time of my engagement it was thought possible
that we would all go abroad together the following
year (but for the Civil War we would have done
so).   But they were very kind and considerate in
releasing me anyway, and did so, they said, for
my own good.

Counselled the doctor, "Get into trade,
my boy! get into trade!   At every opportunity
get into trade!   Trade is the foundation of the
Empire. "

Mr. Dickens, bless his heart, who had
made a date to call at Spa road on another

matter--learning of which, I had arranged for
Dad and Mother to drop in so that it turned out
to be quite a conference--said, "It's all right,
Billy; it's quite the right thing to do; it will
broaden your knowledge to meet great opportunity, you know." The doctor and the mistress,
and Mr. Dickens, and even Ted and Martha promised to patronize me when I "got into trade."

Between the two windows of the second
story of the haberdashery was a sign reading
ESTABLISHED 1783 (anyhow that is how the date
runs in my mind) and as though to give me a
stronger guarantee, there was let into the brick-
work of the wall near the door and about seven
feet high a small shield-shaped brass plate bearing the lettering: THIS ESTABLISHMENT INSURED
BY MANCHESTER UNION FIRE INSURANCE
COMPANY, LTD.   A. D. 1784.   (One would
never know the shield were brass unless he
started one day, as I did to keep up its polish.)

The Establishment was and no doubt is
yet (unless some major improvements have razed
it and that is not likely as it was already a very
wide street) of a dull red brick, three stories to
the parapet with a mansard story above which
contained two rooms.   The front one was mine.
One would not see this mansard roof except from
across the street.   The building was a rod wide
and four and a half long on the ground, and was
hemmed in by other buildings, some lower and
some higher.   The shop room was thirteen by
thirty feet.   (The next time you, dear reader,
are in the Boro, you may verify this survey as
a test of a sixty-five year old memory.)

G. W. C. Cross was one of nature's
noblemen and looked it; he was about seventy-
five and looked that too; he was eccentric in his
ultra-conservatism and deeply-set habits, each
of which was acquired when as a young man he
was commissioned clerk of the parish. He had
never changed one of them nor added another to
them. His virtues were acquired at the same
time as his eccentric habits and remained as
immutable. Among them were courteous tolerance of another's opinions and a charitable view
of another's faults. His religious convictions
were first imbibed with his mother's milk and
they had never curdled. He had listened for
hours at his own request to my Dad's theological
expositions of another faith and his own remained
as adamantine as the foundation of the church
opposite. He was quiet and reserved and did not
argue; he easily sobered any inclination for argument. He expressed no opinions and asked for
none, yet was a good conversationalist and a
pleasant companion. His was a smooth tranquil
life if there ever was one.

And yet, Mr. Cross was afraid of Miss
Esther. I don't know if Miss Esther realized
this; but he was, ludicrously, if the term is not
an improper one to use for one so dignified and
sedate, afraid of Miss Esther. Young as I was,
it gave me the impression that he was always
getting into the jam, or telling fibs, or tearing
his clothes, or saying something naughty. I felt
sure I would not look so afraid if I were doing
such things.

He had seven pairs of boots, a certain
pair for each day of the week, and there were

always six pairs in exact order on a particular
shelf in his boot closet under the stairs. If,
perchance, as I have known it to happen, Monday's
boots were not returned by Monday from the boot-
maker who had them for repairs, then, Monday
was a fretful day, a sorrowful day, a gruesome
day. There was and could be no help for it. But
then no matter what else Monday was it would
not be a creaking day. All of Mr. G. W. C.
Cross' boots creaked whether they were new,
half worn out, or ready for the ragman; they all
creaked and because they creaked they caused him
to tip-toe when afraid of Miss Esther. On such
a Monday with no Monday boots, he just had to
go about in his stockinged feet, that's all there
was to do, and they didn't creak.

      And, if perchance the maid became con-
fused as to the day of the week, and mistakingly
cleaned Thursday's boots on Wednesday morning,
or as to the boot of the day, and shined Saturday's on Monday, and placed them as usual under
his breakfast chair at which he knelt for the eight
o'clock prayer, it would be hard on all of us that
day even though the error could be at once reme-
died. It was particularly hard if this dreadful
mistake were discovered as he knelt there and
as we all knelt at our chairs, for it would then
be the burden of his very long and perfervid
prayer, and only himself and the Almighty, and
we, could know whose sin, whose ingratitude,
whose turpitude, whose deplorably bad employment of heavenly endowed talent he was praying
for. But we knew, or hoped we knew, that who-
ever it were, with such a fervent and just medi-
ator pleading his cause, he or she must surely
be pardoned if there were any charity in heaven.

And we would all say "Amen," perhaps glancing
at the maid on the verge of her Reconciliation.
But this would be the end of it.   Mr. Cross
would on arising pass the boots to the maid with
the gentle remark,   "These are Thursday's, my
dear," get the surprised rely, "Why! Bless me,
sir, I was thinking this <u>was</u> Thursday, sir!" and
the maid would have Wednesday's boots by his
side before breakfast was over.   She was just
as likely, too, to find a loose sixpence in each
Thursday boot next morning.

    The master took fright on one occasion
when,   because he was six feet tall and had long
arms and I, only five feet with short ones, needed
to get a glass chimney down from a hanging
lamp to clean it and asked him to please lift it
down for me.   In doing so he dropped and
smashed it.   With finger on lips and an anxious,
frightened glance rearward, he plunged down to
the bottom of his trouser pocket, and it was a
long way down for it swallowed up his whole arm,
drew forth a sixpence, and in pantomime tip-
toed to the front door, drawing me after him,
also tip-toeing.   Pointing across the street to
an ironmonger's, he said, "There!" and putting
the coin in my hand and trusting to my wits to
understand, added "Run! Quick!"   I ran quick
and got back tip-toe with a new chimney before
he had had time to clear up the debris.   Putting
a polish on the new chimney, he slyly grinned
at me, screwed up one eye to a squint, shook his
head slowly in Miss Esther's direction and gave a
relieved sigh.   Saying never a word.

    That sixpence was not the property of the
till of the establishment, which was in easy

reach--nearer in fact than the bottom of his
trouser pocket.   It was not the property of the
church for that was kept in a dispatch box until
it got within the vault of the vestry.   But it was
out of the personal spending which Miss Esther
allowed him weekly.

CHAPTER XXXV

I must explain here that cross streets in
the Boro were few and far between. It would not
do to let too much pure air and sunshine within
the slums. It would reveal too much. And so,
ingress to and egress from the interior, bewildering maze of narrow, crooked, wretched
alleys I have described as Seven Dials were
through narrow slits (they could not be described
more broadly) between the shop buildings facing
the Boro and likewise facing Union Street.

It is difficult to explain how these slits
originated; most of them were too narrow for
the passage of a vehicle and some were scarcely
a yard wide. There were many stories to account for them; one, which may be as good as
any, was to the effect that under an old Breton
Law, "Any path on private property over which
a corpse and funeral cortege had passed on three
separate occasions, did, thereafter--unless the
path were closed and fenced off or locked for
one year and a public notice displayed--become
a public right-of-way and could not thereafter be
repossessed and built upon."

Sometimes in Mr. Dickens' calls at the
shop his inquiries were in regard to this labyrinth
of vice and then I was called upon for information.

He asked me on one occasion what I thought
about his going through it alone.

I told him, "Not as you are, sir; not
without a PC man or a copper! but if you would
care to make up as a coster, I could take you
through it safely myself, sir."

This risk, however, did not appeal to him,
at least it was not followed. Not from any personal fear of violence, I am sure, because he
must have done a lot of it in his time, but more
likely because the necessity for this sort of
knowledge was for him waning.

I had thoroughly explored this interior
mess in my piratin' days and in my lather boy
days and there was one of these slits, entrees
to Seven Dials, only three shops distant from
our establishment, out of which poured the denizens of the underworld like rats from a burrow.
Much of our patronage came from this source,
which made my previous slum experiences now
useful for trading with it was a case of a wary
eye, a ready wit, and diamond-cut-diamond
sharpness.

These slits were like the threads of a
spider web down which the arachnid comes trundling quickly to its victim. Their entrances were
usually arched over, so that the original owner
of the ground might at least avail himself of the
upper space (if the third corpse and its procession claimed only the ground surface) and this
made each of the slit entrances dark and sinister.
There were spiders in the guise of purse snatch-
ers, dips, and pick-pockets (usually small and

expertly trained boys and alas to relate, sometimes small girls) and in their stealthy forays
and quick retreats with their plunder into these
holes they usually had a confederate concealed
in a doorway or some recess ready, in case of
pursuit, to let pass the thief and trip up the
pursuer.

This trick was known to the peelers and
made them very wary of chasing into these tun-
nels. I knew more about this, possibly, than
did the cops; possibly I was more venturesome
than they; possibly more agile and a better
sprinter; certainly I had had enough practice to
make me so. At any rate, it several times
happened that I detected a snatcher making off
with something from the outside exhibit of our
shop and I immediately gave chase.

For instance: it was fifteen minutes before
prayers at Cross' Haberdashery, my rough chores
were done, and I was behind the counter. I was
about to don my breakfast jacket when I saw a
working-shirt, a part of the outdoor display,
snatched from its place and disappear. It was
done so quickly that I barely saw more than that
the snatcher was a boy of about my own size and
that he was bare-footed. With a yell intended to
warn the rear I leaped the counter and was after
him in a flash, just in time to see him disappear
in a slit only three shops distant. In I dived
after him. Neither of us as it happened this time
was molested in the tunnel and I overtook him
in about a hundred yeards after getting into the
open. I would not have done this, however, if
he had not slowed up. We had already passed a
number of Seven Dials citizens, including some

kids who set up a yelling of jeers, for everyone
knew from experience what was up.

On the lowest of several stone steps of a
hovel we had reached stood a tough looking indi-
vidual who I could have sworn was Bill Sykes, if
I had not known of my own knowledge that Bill
Sykes was hanged; or the ghost of Bill, but if his
ghost, it must have spent a terrible night, judging by its appearance. The snatcher while running had rolled up the shirt and had stuck it in
the waist-band of his trousers, a nice precaution:
having his hands free for eventualities and yet
not parting with his booty. As he slowed up, he
swerved, to get the big ghost between us for his
protection. He appealed to it for help. As I
came up, the big ghost nimbly backed up to the
top step, thus removing its protective cover. At
the speed I was going I had to leap onto the lower
steps immediately in front of it. This gave me
an altitude over my prey so that the next bound
landed me on top of him as he lay upon the cobbles. I could not at the finish have told what
happened next for the next--and the next--and the
next happened very rapidly. I only know that I
expected the big ghost's grasp on my collar as
quickly as it could get to me. But it didn't come.
With the snatcher and myself for the next few
moments there were two souls with but a single
thought and we certainly dwelt upon that thought
as desperately as we were able. There came a
lull for a second in which to draw breath, and
then a hand, a big hand, near, real, impossible
to be a ghost's hand, came past me and wrenched
the booty from the waist-band. I looked up at
him, a moment of St. George and the Dragon,
to see the burly arbiter, very deliberately shaking

out the shirt as if to inspect its workmanship
and to determine the correspondence of button-
holes to buttons.   As hours seemed to pass, he
neatly folded it, rolled it up and reached down
to my collar and hauled me up-end.

With a ghostly moan he roared, "Uh! 'E's
lick't!" And with this illuminating decision he
stuffed the roll of shirt into my waist-band.

I then found myself, except to include the
prostrate form at my feet, the center of a very
jolly and sympathetic crowd which seemed fully
to approve of the adjudication of the big ghost,
who I now found could fluently talk "pid klat" and
who had not moved a muscle except for this official decision.

The sweat was in my eyes; my head (discovered to be of less density than cobbles) was
bleeding; my face was full of alley filth.   But,
oh, I was so happy!

I was vociferously escorted by some of
my audience to the slit where we met a cop whom
standers-by had summoned to the "murder" going
on; seeing there was no use delving any furthur
into the mess, the peeler escorted me to the
haberdashery, where G. W. C. and Miss Esther,
and the maid in the background, received us in
great alarm.

The Majesty of the Law in a proper per-
functory way, asked the owner of the recovered
property if "there were any charges to be brought."
Mr. Cross, in some agitation, repeated this legal
formula to me.

I, being a minor and not qualified to de-
cide, nevertheless did so by saying, "No! No
charge! I lick'd 'im! That's all. See?!" And
I held up the recovered booty, which with its
stains told a story in itself, as exhibit I and I
held forth my bloody face and my two bleeding
hands as exhibits II, III, and IV. And thus did
the preliminary hearing end.

All this, snatch, chase, and recovery,
happened within five minutes and so there was
still some time to eight o'clock prayers. With
the help of a very pale maid, who was sickened
with the gore, I was patched up and down to my
chair on exact time.

I would not for the world have you think I
felt irreverently toward that dear, old, and pious
gentleman, G. W. C., or that he was in the
slightest degree hypocritical, but I did wish I
could have taken down that morning's prayer in
short-hand as Mr. William could have done. It
breathed sincere thankfulness to heaven for our
miraculous escape from a great peril, and gratitude that we were spared to meet another day;
gratitude for the brave defense of our country;
of our homes; of our property; of our honor; of
our peace; gratitude that our defense could so
spontaneously shed its blood in its faithfulness
to duty; that its strength, feeble as it might be,
was all bravely expended in service. I may as
well abbreviate it here but it didn't end that
morning, it simply stopped: to be continued in
our next.

For two reasons: the kipper and the toast
had been dreadfully neglected because of my plight

in the noble defense of property, and the maid
had silently risen and retired guiltily to the
kitchen during the gratitudes.   And my poor head,
which I had favored so far by all sorts of attitudes, had at last given way and sunk to the chair
seat with an audible groan, hearing which, Miss
Esther in great fright and for the first time in
her life, wakened her father from his intense ab-
sorption with the Almighty by crying, "Father!
Father! Harrison is dying! Surely!" and there
was great confusion.   Thus the direct line to the
throne of grace was short-circuited.

It wasn't so bad as feared however, for
with a change of position and a little stimulant,
Harrison was himself again, with appetite in good
order but with a mouth too sore to enjoy it.

There were four distinct human states at
the breakfast table that morning; mine, too chaotic
for immediate analysis; the master's, which had
been static and on its way as such onto the day's
weather chart when it was interrupted, could now
be called "unsettled;" Miss Esther, the maid had
overheard her say, was disgusted with the blood-
thirsty beast (meaning me, thought the maid) but
glad to get back the property of the establishment; and, the maid's own: a bit overcast by the
thundercloud aspect of her mistress yet sufficiently serene to kiss the spot to make it well on
her "brave little hero."

In Seven Dials it was a credit to pull off
an unlawful act such as the one attempted but a
disgrace to be caught at it.   The snatcher would
have been lauded had he escaped me with his booty
but he immediately lost sympathy with his class

when he failed. He and I being fairly matched
as to size, strength, and agility, there was no
disposition to interfere with the battle.

Had I been a man, or especially if I had
been a cop, the ghost would surely have tripped
me up. Had I got the worst of the encounter,
the snatcher would have escaped with praise and
the mob would have jeered me. Due credit had
been awarded me and there was no more snatch-
ing from our shop by the boys of that slit.

Mr. Dickens, with Ted listening, was
afterward told of this affair. His comment to
G. W. C. was "how like the affairs of nations"
and to me, "Save up your fighting, Billy, for
that 'great opportunity."

And from Ted, "A loi a bet ya wallop't
he, Billy!"

CHAPTER XXXVI

Whenever Mr. Dickens drove to or from Gad's Hill and the City he almost had to pass this haberdashery. Its facade, although not so impressive, must have been as familiar to him as was the church across the way. Little Dorrit was then a comparatively fresh publication and through it can be seen the familiarity Dickens must have had with the interior of St. George's Church.

Naturally my master, Mr. Cross, was familiar with it too, knowing its every stone and chink, and as keeper of its records he knew every gravestone in the yard and the inscription on every stone and the history of every decedent, at least of those lying monumented in its upper layer, even though there had been no additions during his lifetime. And he could have gone deeper into its decaying history, for his records told him that the ground, which was from twelve to twenty feet higher than the street level, contained at least three, and rumor had it four, separate tiers of graves, the beginnings of which were more ancient than the present church, but all on record.

Naturally Miss Esther, whose eyes had first opened on a view of the church and whose

babyhood and childhood and maidenhood and spin-
sterhood had been spent in contemplation of its
outside smut and its   inside gloom; whose religion
had been taken in at its font, at its communion
table, at its altar, in its Sunday school; who had
worshipped in its choir; who had witnessed and
helped to officiate at many of its solemn funerals
and joyous weddings; who, naturally, had many
times dreamed and pictured herself standing before the altar saying "I will" to the only man;
naturally she was familiar with it all, even still
dreaming and picturing.

Naturally Mr. William, whose eyes had
first opened ten years after Miss Esther's on the
same view and whose only playground later on
was among the stones in the graveyard (where he
later became   proficient in copying the letters and
inscriptions) and among the pews in the church
nave where his youth was spent as usher and
guide; and where he helped the verger and bell-
ringer in   their duties; and in the vestry where
his beautiful and careful penmanship in the records
from 1850 to 1860 was clearly distinguishable
from the sprawling chirography of his father's--
naturally he, too, was familiar with it all.

And all the Crosses were ardent lovers
of Dickens and his works and felt toward him as
old neighbors.   They knew intimately the many
locations in the neighborhood that he had used for
the scenes of his stories; of his own early home
five minutes away in Lant Street; of the Marshalsea Debtors Prison, less than five minutes
away behind the church and reached by several
of those "slits" I have referred to.   And they
knew the Hide and Leather Market nearby that

prison where myriad black ravens fought with the
rats and strutted and screamed their raucous
cries of "goo' bye, goo' bye!" and "get out, get
out!" among the green hides; and where Saturday
was market day and a gala day and a noisy,
drunken, gorging, fighting day among the slaugh-
tering fraternity, with the tanners and hide deal-
ers and leather merchants and furriers and boot-
makers and saddlers and hair and glue and button
and comb manufacturers from all the kingdom
over and from the continent, to vie with the
ravens in the vociferous barter of pelts.

But despite this close association of environment and faithful reading of his works the
Cross Establishment did not know very much about
the conditions in the immediate vicinity of its own
back yards and which was the real beginning of
Seven Dials. No; not nearly so much as I could
tell them and they had never met Mr. Dickens
personally to speak to him.

When they had learned of my close acquaintance with him and when on needful occasions
Ted would stop at the curb with his master (and
I think they made needful occasions very often
for they would ask for extraordinary things never
stocked at a haberdashery) it naturally came about
that they became acquainted with each other and
G. W. C. would chat with Mr. Dickens while Ted
would chat with me and tell me silly things that
had happened at Gad's Hill and the Lodge and
would slyly slip me a little bouquet which he said
Ruth had sent for my mother (it had come direct
from the gate-keeper of the Lodge and was intended for myself, that's all there was to it) and
while telling me this he kept a ludicrously straight

face which could not however conceal his laughing eyes.

On one occasion Mr. Dickens expressed a wish for prowling in the church "to remind me," he said, "of my own youth and of Little Dorrit and Maggie and old associations." G. W. C. eagerly offered to escort him and at Mr. Dickens' suggestion, invited me to go with them. I had faced the church for a year and had never entered it, although I had frequently wandered in its graveyard.

It was a gloomy day, a bit foggy, and the dew, lingering on the rank and long-neglected grass of the disused cemetery was sending up a vapor in curling wisps, the wraiths of souls. The wide stone flagging leading from the street steps to the church, over which countless wedding processions had decorously passed when St. George's had been the fashionable church of the neighborhood, now had lichen in its crevices and slimy moss on its surface. St. George's popularity had vanished.

It was not a day, nor a scene, for cheerful thoughts. As we advanced inside and to the nave the depression was intense, and when we reached the vestry where Little Dorrit was told she would "find a fire on account of the painters" it seemed as though nothing had been done to it in the way of renewals or refurbishings for hundreds of years--the gloom was beyond expression. And I marvelled to myself how one man had used this room, as official custodian of its records for more than forty years, and yet retained a semblance of human sympathy to say nothing of

much quiet humor and even fits of gaiety. But
this vestry was the hallowed room where our
master had laid his most pathetic scene in Little
Dorrit.

Something perhaps of the morbidness which
it is said prompts the murderer to haunt the
scene of his crime, or of the hopelessness of the
discarded lover in visiting the familiar trysting
tree probably may have occasioned Mr. Dickens'
desire to see this spot again. The sentiment he
had laid upon it must have made it very real to
him. He showed us the very spot where Little
Dorrit and Maggie had slept, on the fearsome
night when they were locked out of the near-by
Marshalsea Prison and he admitted that G. W. C.
might, indeed, have been the very verger, or
whatever he was, who made up their beds from
the pew cushions. And he showed us the very
font where the child Dorrit had been baptised and
then, as though to raise our spirits above the
gloom, he showed us the very spot on the carpet
where she had stood to be happily married.

"Three o'clock, and half-past three, and
they had passed over London Bridge. They had
heard the rush of the tide against obstacles; and
looked down, awed, through the dark vapor on
the river; had seen little spots of lighted water
where the bridge lamps were reflected, shining
like demon eyes, with a terrible fascination in
them for guilt and misery. They had shrunk past
homeless people, lying coiled up in nooks. They
had run from drunkards. They had started from
slinking men, whistling and signing to one another
at bye corners, or running away at full speed.
Though everywhere the leader and the guide, Little

Dorrit, happy for once in her youthful appearance,
feigned to cling to and rely upon Maggie. And
more than once some voice, from among a knot
of brawling or prowling figures in their path, had
called out to the rest, to 'let the woman and the
child go by!'

"So, the woman and the child had gone by,
and gone on, and five had sounded from the
steeples. They were walking slowly towards the
east, already looking for the first pale streaks
of day. *** Going round by the church, she saw
lights there, and the door open; and went up the
steps, and looked in.

" 'Who's that?' cried a stout old man,
who was putting on a night cap as if he were
going to bed in a vault.

" 'It's no one particular, sir,' said Little
Dorrit.

" 'Stop!' cried the man. 'Let's have a
look at you!'

"This caused her to turn back again, in
the act of going out, and to present herself and
her charge before him.

" 'I thought so!' said he. "I know you.'

" 'We have often seen each other,' said
Little Dorrit, recognizing the sexton, or the
beadle, or the verger, or whatever he was, 'when
I have been at church here.'

" 'More than that, we've got your birth in

our Register, you know; you're one of our
curiosities. '

" 'Indeed?' said Little Dorrit.

" 'To be sure. As the child of the--by-
the-bye, how did you get out so early?'

" 'We were shut out last night, and are
waiting to get in. '

" 'You don't mean it? And there's another
hour good yet! Come into the vestry. You'll
find a fire in the vestry, on account of the painters. I'm waiting for the painters, or I shouldn't
be here, you may depend upon it. One of our
curiosities mustn't be cold, when we have it in
our power to warm her up comfortable. Come
along. *** Stay a bit. I'll get some cushions out
of the church and you and your friend shall lie
down before the fire. Don't be afraid of not going
in to join your father when the gate opens. I'll
call you. '

" He soon brought in the cushions, and
strewed them on the ground.

" 'There you are, you see. Again as
large as life. Oh, never mind thanking. I've
daughters of my own. And though they weren't
born in the Marshalsea Prison, they might have
been, if I had been, in my ways of carrying on,
of your father's breed. Stop a bit. I must put
something under the cushion for your head.
Here's a burial volume. Just the thing! ... But
what makes these books interesting to most people
is--not who's in 'em, but who isn't--who's coming,

you know, and when.   That's the interesting
question.

"Commendingly looking back at the pillow
he had improvised, he left them to their hour's
repose. Maggie was snoring already, and Little
Dorrit was soon fast asleep, with her head resting on that sealed book of Fate, untroubled by
the mysterious blank leaves. "